The In 1919

Table of Contents

in 1919

Arthur Ransome

Kessinger Publishing reprints thousands of hard–to–find books!

Visit us at http://www.kessinger.net

PUBLISHER'S NOTE

On August 27, 1914, in London, I made this note in a memorandum book: "Met Arthur Ransome at_____'s; discussed a book on the n's relation to the war in the light of psychological background—folklore." The book was not written but the idea that instinctively came to him pervades his every utterance on things n.

The versatile man who commands more than respect as the biographer of Poe and Wilde; as the (translator of and commentator on Remy de Gourmont; as a folklorist, has shown himself to be consecrated to the truth. The document that Mr. Ransome hurried out of in the early days of the Soviet government (printed in the New Republic and then widely circulated as a pamphlet), was the first notable appeal from a non–n to the American people for fair play in a crisis understood then even less than now.

The British Who's Who—that Almanach de Gotha of people who do things or choose their parents wisely—tells us that Mr. Ransome's recreations are "walking, smoking, fairy stories." It is, perhaps, his intimacy with the last named that enables him to distinguish between myth and fact and that makes his activity as an observer and recorder so valuable in a day of bewilderment and betrayal.

B. W. H.

INTRODUCTION

I am well aware that there is material in this book which will be misused by fools both white and red. That is not my fault. My object has been narrowly limited. I have tried by means of a bald record of conversations and things seen, to provide material for those who wish to know what is being done and thought in Moscow at the present time, and demand something more to go upon than secondhand reports of wholly irrelevant atrocities committed by either one side or the other, and often by neither one side nor the other, but by irresponsible scoundrels who, in the natural turmoil of the greatest convulsion in the history of our civilization, escape temporarily here and there from any kind of control.

The book is in no sense of the word propaganda. For propaganda, for the defence or attack of the Communist position, is needed a knowledge of economics, both from the capitalist and socialist standpoints, to which I cannot pretend. Very many times during the revolution it has seemed to me a tragedy that no Englishman properly equipped in this way was in studying the gigantic experiment which, as a country, we are allowing to pass abused but not examined. I did my best. I got, I think I may say, as near as any foreigner who was not a Communist could get to what was going on. But I never lost the bitter feeling that the opportunities of study which I made for myself were wasted, because I could not hand them on to some other Englishman, whose education and training would have enabled him to make a better, a fuller use of them. Nor would it have been difficult for such a man to get the opportunities which were given to me when, by sheer persistence in enquiry, I had overcome the hostility which I at first encountered as the correspondent of a "bourgeois" newspaper. Such a man could be in now, for the Communists do not regard war as we regard it. The Germans would hardly have allowed an Allied Commission to come to Berlin a year ago to investigate the nature and working of the Autocracy. The ns, on the other hand, immediatelya greed to the suggestion of the Berne Conference that they should admit a party of socialists, the majority of whom, as they well knew, had already expressed condemnation of them. Further, in agreeing to this, they added that they would as willingly admit a committee of enquiry sent by any of the "bourgeois" governments actually at war with them.

I am sure that there will be many in England who will understand much better than I the drudgery of the revolution which is in this book very imperfectly suggested. I repeat that it is not my fault that they must make do with the eyes and ears of an ignorant observer. No doubt I have not asked the questions they would have asked, and have thought interesting and novel much which they would have taken for granted.

The book has no particular form, other than that given it by a more or less accurate adherence to chronology in setting down things seen and heard. It is far too incomplete to allow me to call it a Journal. I think I could have made it twice as long without repetitions, and I am not at all sure that in choosing in a hurry between this and that I did not omit much which could with advantage be substituted for what is here set down. There is nothing here of my talk with the English soldier prisoners and nothing of my visit to the officers confined in the Butyrka Gaol. There is nothing of the plagues of typhus and influenza, or of the desperate situation of a people thus visited and unable to procure from abroad the simplest drugs which they cannot manufacture at home or even the anaesthetics necessary for their wounded on every frontier of their country. I forgot to describe the ballet which I saw a few days before leaving. I have said nothing of the talk I had with Eliava concerning the n plans for the future of Turkestan. I could think of a score of other omissions. Judging from what I have read since my return from , I imagine people will find my book very poor in the matter of Terrors. There is nothing here of the Red Terror, or of any of the Terrors on the other side. But for its poverty in atrocities my book will be blamed only by fanatics, since they alone desire proofs of past Terrors as justification for new ones.

On reading my manuscript through, I find it quite surprisingly dull. The one thing that I should have liked to transmit through it seems somehow to have slipped away. I should have liked to explain what was the appeal of the revolution to men like Colonel Robins and myself, both of us men far removed in origin and upbringing from the revolutionary and socialist movements in our own countries. Of course no one who was able, as we were able, to watch the men of the revolution at close quarters could believe for a moment that they were the mere paid agents of the very power which more than all others represented the stronghold they had set out to destroy. We had the knowledge of the injustice being done to these men to urge us in their defence. But there was more in it than that. There was the feeling, from which we could never escape, of the creative effort of the revolution. There was the thing that distinguishes the creative from other artists, the living, vivifying expression of something hitherto hidden in the consciousness of humanity. If this book were to be an accurate record of my own impressions, all the drudgery, gossip, quarrels, arguments, events and experiences it contains would have to be set against a background of that extraordinary vitality which obstinately persists in Moscow even in these dark days of discomfort, disillusion, pestilence, starvation and unwanted war.

ARTHUR RANSOME.

TO PETROGRAD

On January 30 a party of four newspaper correspondents, two Norwegians, a Swede and myself, left Stockholm to go into . We travelled with the members of the Soviet Government's Legation, headed by Vorovsky and Litvinov, who were going home after the breaking off of official relations by Sweden. Some months earlier I had got leave from the Bolsheviks to go into to get further material for my history of the revolution, but at the last moment there was opposition and it seemed likely that I should be refused permission. Fortunately, however, a copy of the Morning Post reached Stockholm, containing a report of a lecture by Mr. Lockhart in which he had said that as I had been out of for six months I had no right to speak of conditions there. Armed with this I argued that it would be very unfair if I were not allowed to come and see things for myself. I had no further difficulties.

We crossed by boat to Abo, grinding our way through the ice, and then travelled by rail to the n frontier, taking several days over the journey owing to delays variously explained by the Finnish authorities. We were told that the n White Guards had planned an attack on the train. Litvinov, half–smiling, wondered if they were purposely giving time to the White Guards to organize such an attack. Several nervous folk inclined to that opinion. But at Viborg we were told that there were grave disorders in Petrograd and that the Finns did not wish to fling us into the middle of a scrimmage. Then someone obtained a newspaper and we read a detailed account of what was happening. This account was, as I learnt on my return, duly telegraphed to England like much other news of a similar character. There had been a serious revolt in Petrograd. The Semenovsky regiment had gone over to the mutineers, who had seized the town. The Government, however, had escaped to Kronstadt, whence they were bombarding Petrograd with naval guns.

This sounded fairly lively, but there was nothing to be done, so we finished up the chess tournament we had begun on the boat. An Esthonian won it, and I was second, by reason of a lucky win over Litvinov, who is really a better player. By Sunday night we reached Terijoki and on Monday moved slowly to the frontier of Finland close to Bieloostrov. A squad of Finnish soldiers was waiting, excluding everybody from the station and seeing that no dangerous revolutionary should break away on Finnish territory. There were no horses, but three hand sledges were brought, and we piled the luggage on them, and then set off to walk to the frontier duly convoyed by the Finns. A Finnish lieutenant walked at the head of the procession, chatting good—humouredly in Swedish and German, much as a man might think it worth while to be kind to a crowd of unfortunates just about to be flung into a boiling cauldron. We walked a few hundred yards along the line and then turned into a road deep in snow through a little bare wood, and so down to the little wooden bridge over the narrow frozen stream that separates Finland from . The bridge, not twenty yards across, has a toll bar at each end, two sentry boxes and two sentries. On the n side the bar was the familiar black and white of the old n Empire, with a sentry box to match. The Finns seemingly had not yet had time to paint their bar and box.

The Finns lifted their toll bar, and the Finnish officers leading our escort walked solemnly to the middle of the bridge. Then the luggage was dumped there, while we stood watching the trembling of the rickety little bridge under the weight of our belongings, for we were all taking in with us as much food as we decently could. We were none of us allowed on the bridge until an officer and a few men had come down to meet us on the n side. Only little Nina, Vorovskv's daughter, about ten years old, chattering Swedish with the Finns, got leave from them, and shyly, step by step, went down the other side of the bridge and struck up acquaintance with the soldier of the Red Army who stood there, gun in hand, and obligingly bent to show her the sign, set in his hat, of the crossed sickle and hammer of the Peasants' and Workmen's Republic. At last the Finnish lieutenant took the list of his prisoners and called out the names "Vorovsky, wife and one bairn," looking laughingly over his shoulder at Nina flirting with the sentry. Then "Litvinov," and so on through all the ns, about thirty of them. We four visitors, Grimlund the Swede, Puntervald and Stang, the Norwegians, and I, came last. At last, after a general shout of farewell, and "Helse Finland" from Nina, the Finns turned and went back into their civilization, and we went forward into the new struggling civilization of . Crossing that bridge we passed from one philosophy to another, from one extreme of the class struggle to the other, from a dictatorship of the bourgeoisie to a dictatorship of the proletariat.

The contrast was noticeable at once. On the Finnish side of the frontier we had seen the grandiose new frontier station, much larger than could possibly be needed, but quite a good expression of the spirit of the new Finland. On the n side we came to the same grey old wooden station known to all passengers to and from for polyglot profanity and passport difficulties. There were no porters, which was not surprising because there is barbed wire and an extremely hostile sort of neutrality along the frontier and traffic across has practically ceased. In the buffet, which was very cold, no food could be bought. The long tables once laden with caviare and other zakuski were bare. There was, however, a samovar, and we bought tea at sixty kopecks a glass and lumps of sugar at two roubles fifty each. We took our tea into the inner passport room, where I think a stove must have been burning the day before, and there made some sort of a meal off some of Puntervald's Swedish hard–bread. It is difficult to me to express the curious mixture of depression and exhilaration that was given to the party by this derelict starving station combined with the feeling that we were no longer under guard but could do more or less as we liked. It split the party into two factions, of which one wept while the other sang. Madame Vorovsky, who had not been in since the first revolution, frankly wept, but she wept still more in Moscow where she found that even as the wife of a high official of the Government she enjoyed no privileges which would save her from the hardships of the population. But the younger members of the party, together with Litvinov, found their spirits irrepressibly rising in spite of having no dinner. They walked about the village, played with the children, and sang, not revolutionary songs, but just jolly songs, any songs that came into their heads. When at last the train came to take us into Petrograd, and we found that the carriages were unheated, somebody got out a mandoline and we kept ourselves warm by dancing. At the same time I was sorry for the five children who were with us, knowing that a country simultaneously suffering war, blockade and revolution is not a good place for childhood. But they had caught the mood of their parents, revolutionaries going home to their revolution, and trotted excitedly up and down the carriage or anchored themselves momentarily, first on one person's knee and then on another's.

It was dusk when we reached Petrograd. The Finland Station, of course, was nearly deserted, but here there were four porters, who charged two hundred and fifty roubles for shifting the luggage of the party from one end of the platform to the other. We ourselves loaded it into the motor lorry sent to meet us, as at Bieloostrov we had loaded it into the van. There was a long time to wait while rooms were being allotted to us in various hotels, and with several others I walked outside the station to question people about the mutiny and the bombardment of which we had heard in Finland. Nobody knew anything about it. As soon as the rooms were allotted and I knew that I had been lucky enough to get one in the Astoria, I drove off across the frozen river by the Liteini Bridge. The trams were running. The town seemed absolutely quiet, and away down the river I saw once again in the dark, which is never quite dark because of the snow, the dim shape of the fortress, and passed one by one the landmarks I had come to know so well during the last six years–the Summer Garden, the British Embassy, and the great Palace Square where I

7

had seen armoured cars flaunting about during the July rising, soldiers camping during the hysterical days of the Kornilov affair and, earlier, Kornilov himself reviewing the Junkers. My mind went further back to the March revolution, and saw once more the picket fire of the revolutionaries at the corner that night when the remains of the Tzar's Government were still frantically printing proclamations ordering the people to go home, at the very moment while they themselves were being besieged in the Admiralty. Then it flung itself further back still, to the day of the declaration of war, when I saw this same square filled with people, while the Tzar came out for a moment on the Palace balcony. By that time we were pulling up at the Astoria and I had to turn my mind to something else.

The Astoria is now a bare barrack of a place, but comparatively clean. During the war and the first part of the revolution it was tenanted chiefly by officers, and owing to the idiocy of a few of these at the time of the first revolution in shooting at a perfectly friendly crowd of soldiers and sailors, who came there at first with no other object than to invite the officers to join them, the place was badly smashed up in the resulting scrimmage. I remember with Major Scale fixing up a paper announcing the fall of Bagdad either the night this happened or perhaps the night before. People rushed up to it, thinking it some news about the revolution, and turned impatiently away. All the damage has been repaired, but the red carpets have gone, perhaps to make banners, and many of the electric lights were not burning, probably because of the shortage in electricity. I got my luggage upstairs to a very pleasant room on the fourth floor. Every floor of that hotel had its memories for me. In this room lived that brave reactionary officer who boasted that he had made a raid on the Bolsheviks and showed little Madame Kollontai's hat as a trophy. In this I used to listen to Perceval Gibbon when he was talking about how to write short stories and having influenza. There was the room where Miss Beatty used to give tea to tired revolutionaries and to still more tired enquirers into the nature of revolution while she wrote the only book that has so far appeared which gives anything like a true impresionist picture of those unforgettable days.* [(*)"The Red Heart of ."] Close by was the room where poor Denis Garstin used to talk of the hunting he would have when the war should come to an end.

I enquired for a meal, and found that no food was to be had in the hotel, but they could supply hot water. Then, to get an appetite for sleep, I went out for a short walk, though I did not much like doing so with nothing but an English passport, and with no papers to show that I had any right to be there. I had, like the other foreigners, been promised such papers but had not yet received them. I went round to the Regina, which used to be one of the best hotels in the town, but those of us who had rooms there were complaining so bitterly that I did not stay with them, but went off along the Moika to the Nevsky and so back to my own hotel. The streets, like the hotel, were only half lit, and hardly any of the houses had a lighted window. In the old sheepskin coat I had worn on the front and in my high fur hat, I felt like some ghost of the old regime visiting a town long dead. The silence and emptiness of the streets contributed to this effect. Still, the few people I met or passed were talking cheerfully together and the rare sledges and motors had comparatively good roads, the streets being certainly better swept and cleaned than they have been since the last winter of the n Empire.

SMOLNI

Early in the morning I got tea, and a bread card on which I was given a very small allowance of brown bread, noticeably better in quality than the compound of clay and straw which made me ill in Moscow last summer. Then I went to find Litvinov, and set out with him to walk to the Smolni institute, once a school for the daughters of the aristocracy, then the headquarters of the Soviet, then the headquarters of the Soviet Government, and finally, after the Government's evacuation to Moscow, bequeathed to the Northern Commune and the Petrograd Soviet. The town, in daylight, seemed less deserted, though it was obvious that the "unloading" of the Petrograd population, which was unsuccessfully attempted during the Kerensky regime, had been accomplished to a large extent. This has been partly the result of famine and of the stoppage of factories, which in its turn is due to the impossibility of bringing fuel and raw material to Petrograd. A very large proportion of n factory hands have not, as in other countries, lost their connection with their native villages. There was always a considerable annual migration backwards and forwards between the villages and the town, and great numbers of workmen have gone home, carrying with them the ideas of the revolution. It should also be remembered that the bulk of the earlier formed units of the Red Army is composed of workmen from the towns who, except in the case of peasants mobilized in districts which have experienced an occupation by the counter–revolutionaries, are more determined and better understand the need for discipline than the men from the country.

The most noticeable thing in Petrograd to anyone returning after six months' absence is the complete disappearance of armed men. The town seems to have returned to a perfectly peaceable condition in the sense that the need for revolutionary patrols has gone. Soldiers walking about no longer carry their rifles, and the picturesque figures of the revolution who wore belts of machine–gun cartridges slung about their persons have gone.

The second noticeable thing, especially in the Nevsky, which was once crowded with people too fashionably dressed, is the general lack of new clothes. I did not see anybody wearing clothes that looked less than two years old, with the exception of some officers and soldiers who are as well equipped nowadays as at the beginning of the war. Petrograd ladies were particularly fond of boots, and of boots there is an extreme shortage. I saw one young woman in a well–preserved, obviously costly fur coat, and beneath it straw shoes with linen wrappings.

We had started rather late, so we took a train half–way up the Nevsky. The tram conductors are still women. The price of tickets has risen to a rouble, usually, I noticed, paid in stamps. It used to be ten kopecks.

The armoured car which used to stand at the entrance of Smolni has disappeared and been replaced by a horrible statue of Karl Marx, who stands, thick and heavy, on a stout pedestal, holding behind him an enormous top–hat like the muzzle of an eighteen–inch gun. The only signs of preparations for defence that remain are the pair of light field guns which, rather the worse for weather, still stand under the pillars of the portico which they would probably shake to pieces if ever they should be fired. Inside the routine was as it used to be, and when I turned down the passage to get my permit to go upstairs, I could hardly believe that I had been away for so long. The place is emptier than it was. There is not the same eager crowd of country delegates pressing up and down the corridors and collecting literature from the stalls that I used to see in the old days when the serious little workman from the Viborg side stood guard over Trotsky's door, and from the alcove with its window looking down into the great hall, the endless noise of debate rose from the Petrograd Soviet that met below.

Litvinov invited me to have dinner with the Petrograd Commissars, which I was very glad to do, partly because I was hungry and partly because I thought it would be better to meet Zinoviev thus than in any other manner, remembering how sourly he had looked upon me earlier in the revolution. Zinoviev is a Jew, with a lot of hair, a round smooth face, and a very abrupt manner. He was against the November Revolution, but when it had been accomplished returned to his old allegiance to Lenin and, becoming President of the Northern Commune, remained in Petrograd when the Government moved to Moscow. He is neither an original thinker nor a good orator except in debate, in answering opposition, which he does with extreme skill. His nerve was badly shaken by the murders of his friends Volodarsky and Uritzky last year, and he is said to have lost his head after the attack on Lenin, to whom he is extremely devoted. I have heard many Communists attribute to this fact the excesses which followed that event in Petrograd. I have never noticed anything that would make me consider him pro–German, though of course he is pro–Marx. He has, however, a decided prejudice against the English. He was among the Communists who put difficulties in my way as a "bourgeois journalist" in the earlier days of the revolution, and I had heard that he had expressed suspicion and disapproval of Radek's intimacy with me.

I was amused to see his face when he came in and saw me sitting at the table. Litvinov introduced me to him, very tactfully telling him of Lockhart's attack upon me, whereupon he became quite decently friendly, and said that if I could stay a few days in Petrograd on my way back from Moscow he would see that I had access to the historical material I wanted, about the doings of the Petrograd Soviet during the time I had been away. I told him I was surprised to find him here and not at Kronstadt, and asked about the mutiny and the treachery of the Semenovsky regiment. There was a shout of laughter, and Pozern explained that there was no Semenovsky regiment in existence, and that the manufacturers of the story, every word of which was a lie, had no doubt tried to give realism to it by putting in the name of the regiment which had taken a chief part in putting down the Moscow insurrection of fourteen years ago. Pozern, a thin, bearded man, with glasses, was sitting at the other end of the table, as Military Commissar of the Northern Commune.

Dinner in Smolni was the same informal affair that it was in the old days, only with much less to eat. The Commissars, men and women, came in from their work, took their places, fed and went back to work again, Zinoviev in particular staying only a few minutes. The meal was extremely simple, soup with shreds of horseflesh in it, very good indeed, followed by a little kasha together with small slabs of some sort of white stuff of no particular consistency or taste. Then tea and a lump of sugar. The conversation was mostly about the chances of peace, and Litvinov's rather pessimistic reports were heard with disappointment. Just as I had finished, Vorovsky, Madame Vorovsky and little Nina, together with the two Norwegians and the Swede, came in. I learnt that about half the party were going on to Moscow that night and, deciding to go with them, hurried off to the hotel.

PETROGRAD TO MOSCOW

There was, of course, a dreadful scrimmage about getting away. Several people were not ready at the last minute. Only one motor was obtainable for nine persons with their light luggage, and a motor lorry for the heavy things. I chose to travel on the lorry with the luggage and had a fine bumpity drive to the station, reminding me of similar though livelier experiences in the earlier days of the revolution when lorries were used for the transport of machine guns, red guards, orators, enthusiasts of all kinds, and any stray persons who happened to clamber on.

At the Nikolai Station we found perfect order until we got into our wagon, an old third-class wagon, in which a certain number of places which one of the party had reserved had been occupied by people who had no right to be there. Even this difficulty was smoothed out in a manner that would have been impossible a year or even six months ago.

The wagon was divided by a door in the middle. There were open coup=82s and side seats which became plank beds when necessary. We slept in three tiers on the bare boards. I had a very decent place on the second tier, and, by a bit of good luck, the topmost bench over my head was occupied only by luggage, which gave me room to climb up there and sit more or less upright under the roof with my legs dangling above the general tumult of mothers, babies, and Bolsheviks below. At each station at which the train stopped there was a general procession backwards and forwards through the wagon. Everybody who had a kettle or a coffee-pot or a tin can, or even an empty meat tin, crowded through the carriage and out to get boiling water. I had nothing but a couple of thermos flasks, but with these I joined the others. >From every carriage on the train people poured out and hurried to the taps. No one controlled the taps but, with the instinct for co-operation for which ns are remarkable, people formed themselves automatically into queues, and by the time the train started again everybody was back in his place and ready for a general tea-drinking. This performance was repeated again and again throughout the night. People dozed off to sleep, woke up, drank more tea, and joined in the various conversations that went on in different parts of the carriage. Up aloft, I listened first to one and then to another. Some were grumbling at the price of food. Others were puzzling why other nations insisted on being at war with them. One man said he was a co–operator who had come by roundabout ways from Archangel, and describing the discontent there, told a story which I give as an illustration of the sort of thing that is being said in by non–Bolsheviks. This man, in spite of the presence of many Communists in the carriage, did not disguise his hostility to their theories and practice, and none the less told this story. He said that some of the n troops in the Archangel district refused to go to the front. Their commanders, unable to compel them, resigned and were replaced by others who, since the men persisted in refusal, appealed for help. The barracks, so he said, were then surrounded by American troops, and the ns, who had refused to go to the front to fire on other ns, were given the choice, either that every tenth man should be shot, or that they should give up their ringleaders. The ringleaders, twelve in number, were given up, were made to dig their own graves, and shot. The whole story may well be Archangel gossip. If so, as a specimen of such gossip, it is not without significance. In another part of the carriage an argument on the true nature of selfishness caused some heat because the disputants insisted on drawing their illustrations from each other's conduct. Then there was the diversion of a swearing match at a wayside station between the conductor and some one who tried to get into this carriage and should have got into another. Both were fluent and imaginative swearers, and even the man from Archangel stopped talking to listen to them. One, I remember, prayed vehemently that the other's hand might fly off, and the other, not to be outdone, retorted with a similar prayer with regard to the former's head. In England the dispute, which became very fierce indeed, would have ended in assault, but here it ended in nothing but the collection on the platform of a small crowd of experts in bad language who applauded verbal hits with impartiality and enthusiasm.

At last I tried to sleep, but the atmosphere in the carriage, of smoke, babies, stale clothes, and the peculiar smell of the n peasantry which no one who has known it can forget, made sleep impossible. But I travelled fairly comfortably, resolutely shutting my ears to the talk, thinking of fishing in England, and shifting from one bone to another as each ached in turn from contact with the plank on which I lay.

FIRST DAYS IN MOSCOW

It was a rare cold day when I struggled through the crowd out of the station in Moscow, and began fighting with the sledge–drivers who asked a hundred roubles to take me to the Metropole. I remembered coming here a year ago with Colonel Robins, when we made ten roubles a limit for the journey and often travelled for eight. To–day, after heated bargaining, I got carried with no luggage but a typewriter for fifty roubles. The streets were white with deep snow, less well cleaned than the Petrograd streets of this year but better cleaned than the Moscow streets of last year. The tramways were running. There seemed to be at least as many sledges as usual, and the horses were in slightly better condition than last summer when they were scarcely able to drag themselves along. I asked the reason of the improvement, and the driver told me the horses]26]were now rationed like human beings, and all got a small allowance of oats. There were crowds of people about, but the numbers of closed shops were very depressing. I did not then know that this was due to the nationalization of trade and a sort of general stock–taking, the object of which was to prevent profiteering in manufactured goods, etc., of which there were not enough to go round. Before I left many shops were being reopened as national concerns, like our own National Kitchens. Thus, one would see over a shop the inscription, "The 5th Boot Store of the Moscow Soviet" or "The 3rd Clothing Store of the Moscow Soviet" or "The 11th Book Shop." It had been found that speculators bought, for example, half a dozen overcoats, and sold them to the highest bidders, thus giving the rich an advantage over the poor. Now if a man needs a new suit he has to go in his rags to his House Committee, and satisfy them that he really needs a new suit for himself. He is then given the right to buy a suit. In this way an attempt is made to prevent speculation and to ensure a more or less equitable distribution of the inadequate stocks. My greatest surprise was given me by the Metropole itself, because the old wounds of the revolution, which were left unhealed all last summer, the shell–holes and bullet splashes which marked it when I was here before, have been repaired.

Litvinov had given me a letter to Karakhan of the Commissariat of Foreign Affairs, asking him to help me in getting a room. I found him at the Metropole, still smoking as it were the cigar of six months ago. Karakhan, a handsome Armenian, elegantly bearded and moustached, once irreverently described by Radek as "a donkey of classical beauty," who has consistently used such influence as he has in favour of moderation and agreement with the Allies, greeted me very cordially, and told me that the foreign visitors were to be housed in the Kremlin. I told him I should much prefer to live in an hotel in the ordinary way, and he at once set about getting a room for me. This was no easy business, though he obtained an authorization from Sverdlov, president of the executive committee, for me to live where I wished, in the Metropole or the National, which are mostly reserved for Soviet delegates, officials and members of the Executive Committee. Both were full, and he finally got me a room in the old Loskutnaya Hotel, now the Red Fleet, partially reserved for sailor delegates and members of the Naval College.

Rooms are distributed on much the same plan as clothes. Housing is considered a State monopoly, and a general census of housing accommodation has taken place. In every district there are housing committees to whom people wanting rooms apply. They work on the rough and ready theory that until every man has one room no one has a right to two. An Englishman acting as manager of works near Moscow told me that part of his house had been allotted to workers in his factory, who, however, were living with him amicably, and had, I think, allowed him to choose which rooms he should concede. This plan has, of course, proved very hard on house–owners, and in some cases the new tenants have made a horrible mess of the houses, as might, indeed, have been expected, seeing that they had previously been of those who had suffered directly from the decivilizing influences of overcrowding. After talking for some time we went round the corner to the Commissariat for Foreign Affairs, where we found Chicherin who, I thought, had aged a good deal and was (though this was perhaps his manner) less cordial than Karakhan. He asked about England, and I told him Litvinov knew more about that than I, since he had been there more recently. He asked what I thought would be the effect of his Note with detailed terms published that day. I told him that Litvinov, in an interview which I had telegraphed, had mentioned somewhat similar terms some time before, and that personally I doubted whether the Allies would at present come to any agreement with the Soviet Government, but that, if the Soviet Government lasted, my personal opinion was that the commercial isolation of so vast a country as could hardly be prolonged indefinitely on that account alone. (For the general attitude to that Note, see page 44.)

I then met Voznesensky (Left Social Revolutionary), of the Oriental Department, bursting with criticism of the Bolshevik attitude towards his party. He secured a ticket for me to get dinner in the Metropole. This ticket I had to surrender when I got a room in the National. The dinner consisted of a plate of soup, and a very small portion of something else. There are National Kitchens in different parts of the town supplying similar meals. Glasses of weak tea were sold at 30 kopecks each, without sugar. My sister had sent me a small bottle of saccharine just before I left Stockholm, and it was pathetic to see the childish delight with which some of my friends drank glasses of sweetened tea.

The in 1919

>From the Metropole I went to the Red Fleet to get my room fixed up. Six months ago there were comparatively clean rooms here, but the sailors have demoralized the hotel and its filth is indescribable. There was no heating and very little light. A samovar left after the departure of the last visitor was standing on the table, together with some dirty curl–papers and other rubbish. I got the waiter to clean up more or less, and ordered a new samovar. He could not supply spoon, knife, or fork, and only with great difficulty was persuaded to lend me glasses.

The telephone, however, was working, and after tea I got into touch with Madame Radek, who had moved from the Metropole into the Kremlin. I had not yet got a pass to the Kremlin, so she arranged to meet me and get a pass for me from the Commandant. I walked through the snow to the white gate at the end of the bridge which leads over the garden up a steep incline to the Kremlin. Here a fire of logs was burning, and three soldiers were sitting around it. Madame Radek was waiting for me, warming her hands at the fire, and we went together into the citadel of the republic.

A meeting of the People's Commissars was going on in the Kremlin, and on an open space under the ancient churches were a number of motors black on the snow. We turned to the right down the Dvortzovaya street, between the old Cavalier House and the Potyeshny Palace, and went in through a door under the archway that crosses the road, and up some dark flights of stairs to a part of the building that used, I think, to be called the Pleasure Palace. Here, in a wonderful old room, hung with Gobelins tapestries absolutely undamaged by the revolution, and furnished with carved chairs, we found the most incongruous figure of the old Swiss internationalist, Karl Moor, who talked with affection of Keir Hardie and of Hyndman, "in the days when he was a socialist," and was disappointed to find that I knew so little about them. Madame Radek asked, of course, for the latest news of Radek, and I told her that I had read in the Stockholm papers that he had gone to Brunswick, and was said to be living in the palace there.* [(*)It was not till later that we learned he had returned to Berlin, been arrested, and put in prison.] She feared he might have been in Bremen when that town was taken by the Government troops, and did not believe he would ever get back to . She asked me, did I not feel already (as indeed I did) the enormous difference which the last six months had made in strengthening the revolution. I asked after old acquaintances, and learnt that Pyatakov, who, when I last saw him, was praying that the Allies should give him machine rifles to use against the Germans in the Ukraine, had been the first President of the Ukrainian Soviet Republic, but had since been replaced by Rakovsky. It had been found that the

16

views of the Pyatakov government were further left than those of its supporters, and so Pyatakov had given way to Rakovsky who was better able to conduct a more moderate policy. The Republic had been proclaimed in Kharkov, but at that time Kiev was still in the hands of the Directorate.

That night my room in the Red Fleet was so cold that I went to bed in a sheepskin coat under rugs and all possible bedclothes with a mattress on the top. Even so I slept very badly.

The next day I spent in vain wrestlings to get a better room. Walking about the town I found it dotted with revolutionary sculptures, some very bad, others interesting, all done in some haste and set up for the celebrations of the anniversary of the revolution last November. The painters also had been turned loose to do what they could with the hoardings, and though the weather had damaged many of their pictures, enough was left to show what an extraordinary carnival that had been. Where a hoarding ran along the front of a house being repaired the painters had used the whole of it as a vast canvas on which they had painted huge symbolic pictures of the revolution. A whole block in the Tverskaya was so decorated. Best, I think, were the row of wooden booths almost opposite the Hotel National in the Okhotnia Ryadi. These had been painted by the futurists or kindred artists, and made a really delightful effect, their bright colours and naif patterns seeming so natural to Moscow that I found myself wondering how it was that they had never been so painted before. They used to be a uniform dull yellow. Now, in clear primary colours, blue, red, yellow, with rough flower designs, on white and chequered back-grounds, with the masses of snow in the road before them, and bright-kerchiefed women and peasants in ruddy sheepskin coats passing by, they seemed less like futurist paintings than like some traditional survival, linking new Moscow with the Middle Ages. It is perhaps interesting to note that certain staid purists in the Moscow Soviet raised a protest while I was there against the license given to the futurists to spread themselves about the town, and demanded that the art of the revolution should be more comprehensible and less violent. These criticisms, however, did not apply to the row of booths which were a pleasure to me every time I passed them.

In the evening I went to see Reinstein in the National. Reinstein is a little old grandfather, a member of the American Socialist Labour Party, who was tireless in helping the Americans last year, and is a prodigy of knowledge about the revolution. He must be nearly seventy, never misses a meeting of the Moscow Soviet or the Executive

Committee, gets up at seven in the morning, and goes from one end of Moscow to the other to lecture to the young men in training as officers for the Soviet Army, more or less controls the English soldier war prisoners, about whose Bolshevism he is extremely pessimistic, and enjoys an official position as head of the quite futile department which prints hundred–weight upon hundred–weight of propaganda in English, none of which by any chance ever reaches these shores. He was terribly disappointed that I had brought no American papers with me. He complained of the lack of transport, a complaint which I think I must have heard at least three times a day from different people the whole time I was in Moscow. Politically, he thought, the position could not be better, though economically it was very bad. When they had corn, as it were, in sight, they could not get it to the towns for lack of locomotives. These economic difficulties were bound to react sooner or later on the political position.

He talked about the English prisoners. The men are brought to Moscow, where they are given special passports and are allowed to go anywhere they like about the town without convoy of any kind. I asked about the officers, and he said that they were in prison but given everything possible, a member of the International Red Cross, who worked with the Americans when they were here, visiting them regularly and taking in parcels for them. He told me that on hearing in Moscow that some sort of fraternization was going on on the Archangel front, he had hurried off there with two prisoners, one English and one American. With some difficulty a meeting was arranged. Two officers and a sergeant from the Allied side and Reinstein and these two prisoners from the n, met on a bridge midway between the opposing lines. The conversation seemed to have been mostly an argument about working–class conditions in America, together with reasons why the Allies should go home and leave alone. Finally the Allied representatives (I fancy Americans) asked Reinstein to come with them to Archangel and state his case, promising him safe conduct there and back. By this time two ns had joined the group, and one of them offered his back as a desk, on which a safe–conduct for Reinstein was written. Reinstein, who showed me the safe–conduct, doubted its validity, and said that anyhow he could not have used it without instructions from Moscow. When it grew dusk they prepared to separate. The officers said to the prisoners, "What? Aren't you coming back with us?" The two shook their heads decidedly, and said, "No, thank you."

I learnt that some one was leaving the National next day to go to Kharkov, so that I should probably be able to get a room. After drinking tea with Reinstein till pretty late, I went home, burrowed into a mountain of all sorts of clothes, and slept a little.

The in 1919

In the morning I succeeded in making out my claim to the room at the National, which turned out to be a very pleasant one, next door to the kitchen and therefore quite decently warm. I wasted a lot of time getting my stuff across. Transport from one hotel to the other, though the distance is not a hundred yards, cost forty roubles. I got things straightened out, bought some books, and prepared a list of the material needed and the people I wanted to see.

The room was perfectly clean. The chamber—maid who came in to tidy up quite evidently took a pride in doing her work properly, and protested against my throwing matches on the floor. She said she had been in the hotel since it was opened. I asked her how she liked the new regime. She replied that there was not enough to eat, but that she felt freer.

In the afternoon I went downstairs to the main kitchens of the hotel, where there is a permanent supply of hot water. One enormous kitchen is set apart for the use of people living in the hotel. Here I found a crowd of people, all using different parts of the huge stove. There was an old grey—haired Cossack, with a scarlet tunic under his black, wide—skirted, narrow—waisted coat, decorated in the Cossack fashion with ornamental cartridges. He was warming his soup, side by side with a little Jewess making potato—cakes. A spectacled elderly member of the Executive Committee was busy doing something with a little bit of meat. Two little girls were boiling potatoes in old tin cans. In another room set apart for washing a sturdy little long—haired revolutionary was cleaning a shirt. A woman with her hair done up in a blue handkerchief was very carefully ironing a blouse. Another was busy stewing sheets, or something of that kind, in a big cauldron. And all the time people from all parts of the hotel were coming with their pitchers and pans, from fine copper kettles to disreputable empty meat tins, to fetch hot water for tea. At the other side of the corridor was a sort of counter in front of a long window opening into yet another kitchen. Here there was a row of people waiting with their own saucepans and plates, getting their dinner allowances of soup and meat in exchange for tickets. I was told that people thought they got slightly more if they took their food in this way straight from the kitchen to their own rooms instead of being served in the restaurant. But I watched closely, and decided it was only superstition. Besides, I had not got a saucepan.

On paying for my room at the beginning of the week I was given a card with the days of the week printed along its edge. This card gave me the right to buy one dinner daily, and when I bought it that day of the week was snipped off the card so that I could not buy another. The meal consisted of a plate of very good soup, together with a second course of a scrap of meat or fish. The price of the meal varied between five and seven roubles.

One could obtain this meal any time between two and seven. Living hungrily through the morning, at two o'clock I used to experience definite relief in the knowledge that now at any moment I could have my meal. Feeling in this way less hungry, I used then to postpone it hour by hour, and actually dined about five or six o'clock. Thinking that I might indeed have been specially favoured I made investigations, and found that the dinners supplied at the public feeding houses (the equivalent of our national kitchens) were of precisely the same size and character, any difference between the meals depending not on the food but on the cook.

A kind of rough and ready co-operative system also obtained. One day there was a notice on the stairs that those who wanted could get one pot of jam apiece by applying to the provisioning committee of the hotel. I got a pot of jam in this way, and on a later occasion a small quantity of Ukrainian sausage.

Besides the food obtainable on cards it was possible to buy, at ruinous prices, food from speculators, and an idea of the difference in the prices may be obtained from the following examples: Bread is one rouble 20 kopecks per pound by card and 15 to 20 roubles per pound from the speculators. Sugar is 12 roubles per pound by card, and never less than 50 roubles per pound in the open market. It is obvious that abolition of the card system would mean that the rich would have enough and the poor nothing. Various methods have been tried in the effort to get rid of speculators whose high profits naturally decrease the willingness of the villages to sell bread at less abnormal rates. But as a Communist said to me, "There is only one way to get rid of speculation, and that is to supply enough on the card system. When People can buy all they want at 1 rouble 20 they are not going to pay an extra 14 roubles for the encouragement of speculators." "And when will you be able to do that?" I asked. "As soon as the war ends, and we can use our transport for peaceful purposes."

There can be no question about the starvation of Moscow. On the third day after my arrival in Moscow I saw a man driving a sledge laden with, I think, horseflesh, mostly bones, probably dead sledge horses. As he drove a black crowd of crows followed the sledge and perched on it, tearing greedily at the meat. He beat at them continually with his whip, but they were so famished that they took no notice whatever. The starving crows used even to force their way through the small ventilators of the windows in my hotel to pick up any scraps they could find inside. The pigeons, which formerly crowded the streets, utterly undismayed by the traffic, confident in the security given by their supposed connection with religion, have completely disappeared.

Nor can there be any question about the cold. I resented my own sufferings less when I found that the State Departments were no better off than other folk. Even in the Kremlin I found the Keeper of the Archives sitting at work in an old sheepskin coat and felt boots, rising now and then to beat vitality into his freezing hands like a London cabman of old times.

THE EXECUTIVE COMMITTEE ON THE REPLY TO THE PRINKIPO PROPOSAL

February 10th.

It will be remembered that a proposal was made by the Peace Conference that the various de facto governments of should meet on an island in the Bosphorus to discuss matters, an armistice being arranged meanwhile. No direct invitation was sent to the Soviet Government. After attempting to obtain particulars through the editor of a French socialist paper, Chicherin on February 4th sent a long note to the Allies. The note was not at first considered with great favour in , although it was approved by the opposition parties on the right, the Mensheviks even going so far as to say that in sending such a note, the Bolsheviks were acting in the interest of the whole of the n people. The opposition on the left complained that it was a betrayal of the revolution into the hands of the Entente, and there were many Bolsheviks who said openly that they thought it went a little too far in the way of concession. On February 10th, the Executive Committee met to consider the international position.

Before proceeding to an account of that meeting, it will be well to make a short summary of the note in question. Chicherin, after referring to the fact that no invitation had been addressed to them and that the absence of a reply from them was being treated as the rejection of a proposal they had never received, said that in spite of its more and more favourable position, the n Soviet Government considered a cessation of hostilities so desirable that it was ready immediately to begin negotiations, and, as it had more than once declared, to secure agreement "even at the cost of serious concessions in so far as these should not threaten the development of the Republic." "Taking into consideration that the enemies against whom it has to struggle borrow their strength of resistance exclusively from the help shown them by the powers of the Entente, and that therefore these powers are the only actual enemy of the n Soviet Government, the latter addresses itself precisely to the powers of the Entente, setting out the points on which it considers such concessions possible with a view to the ending of every kind of conflict with the aforesaid powers." There follows a list of the concessions they are prepared to make. The first of these is recognition of their debts, the interest on which, "in view of 's difficult financial position and her unsatisfactory credit," they propose to guarantee in raw materials. Then, "in view of the interest continually expressed by foreign capital in the question of the exploitation for its advantage of the natural resources of , the Soviet Government is ready to give to subjects of the powers of the Entente mineral, timber and other concessions, to be defined in detail, on condition that the economic and social structure of Soviet shall not be touched by the internal arrangements of these concessions." The last point is that which roused most opposition. It expresses a willingness to negotiate even concerning such annexations, hidden or open, as the Allies may have in mind. The words used are "The n Soviet Government has not the intention of excluding at all costs consideration of the question of annexations, etc. . . ." Then, "by annexations must be understood the retention on this or that part of the territory of what was the n Empire, not including Poland and Finland, of armed forces of the Entente or of such forces as are maintained by the governments of the Entente or enjoy their financial, military, technical or other support." There follows a statement that the extent of the concessions will depend on the military position. Chicherin proceeds to give a rather optimistic account of the external and internal situation. Finally he touches on the question of propaganda. "The n Soviet Government, while pointing out that it cannot limit the freedom of the revolutionary press, declares its readiness, in case of necessity to include in the general agreement with the powers of the Entente the obligation not to interfere in their internal affairs." The note ends thus: "On the foregoing bases the n Soviet Government is ready immediately to begin negotiations either on Prinkipo island or in any other place whatsoever with all the powers of the Entente together or with separate powers of their number, or with any n political groupings whatsoever, according to the wishes of the powers of the Entente. The n Soviet Government begs the powers of the Entente immediately to inform it whither to send its representatives, and precisely when and by what route." This note was dated February 4th, and was sent out by wireless.

The in 1919

>From the moment when the note appeared in the newspapers of February 5th, it had been the main subject of conversation. Every point in it was criticized and counter–criticized, but even its critics, though anxious to preserve their criticism as a basis for political action afterwards, were desperately anxious that it should meet with a reply. No one in Moscow at that time could have the slightest misgiving about the warlike tendencies of the revolution. The overwhelming mass of the people and of the revolutionary leaders want peace, and only continued warfare forced upon them could turn their desire for peace into desperate, resentful aggression. Everywhere I heard the same story: "We cannot get things straight while we have to fight all the time." They would not admit it, I am sure, but few of the Soviet leaders who have now for eighteen months been wrestling with the difficulties of European have not acquired, as it were in spite of themselves, a national, domestic point of view. They are thinking less about world revolution than about getting bread to Moscow, or increasing the output of textiles, or building river power–stations to free the northern industrial district from its dependence on the distant coal–fields. I was consequently anxious to hear what the Executive Committee would have to say, knowing that there I should listen to some expression of the theoretical standpoint from which my hard–working friends had been drawn away by interests nearer home.

The Executive Committee met as usual in the big hall of the Hotel Metropole, and it met as usual very late. The sitting was to begin at seven, and, foolishly thinking that ns might have changed their nature in the last six months, I was punctual and found the hall nearly empty, because a party meeting of the Communists in the room next door was not finished. The hall looked just as it used to look, with a red banner over the presidium and another at the opposite end, both inscribed "The All n Executive Committee," "Proletariat of all lands, unite," and so on. As the room gradually filled, I met many acquaintances.

Old Professor Pokrovsky came in, blinking through his spectacles, bent a little, in a very old coat, with a small black fur hat, his hands clasped together, just as, so I have been told, he walked unhappily to and fro in the fortress at Brest during the second period of the negotiations. I did not think he would recognize me, but he came up at once, and reminded me of the packing of the archives at the time when it seemed likely that the Germans would take Petrograd. He told me of a mass of material they are publishing about the origin of the war. He said that England came out of it best of anybody, but that France and showed in a very bad light.

Just then, Demian Bledny rolled in, fatter than he used to be (admirers from the country send him food) with a round face, shrewd laughing eyes, and cynical mouth, a typical peasant, and the poet of the revolution. He was passably shaved, his little yellow moustache was trimmed, he was wearing new leather breeches, and seemed altogether a more prosperous poet than the untidy ruffian I first met about a year or more ago before his satirical poems in Pravda and other revolutionary papers had reached the heights of popularity to which they have since attained. In the old days before the revolution in Petrograd he used to send his poems to the revolutionary papers. A few were published and scandalized the more austere and serious−minded revolutionaries, who held a meeting to decide whether any more were to be printed. Since the revolution, he has rapidly come into his own, and is now a sort of licensed jester, flagellating Communists and non−Communists alike. Even in this assembly he had about him a little of the manner of Robert Burns in Edinburgh society. He told me with expansive glee that they had printed two hundred and fifty thousand of his last book, that the whole edition was sold in two weeks, and that he had had his portrait painted by a real artist. It is actually true that of his eighteen different works, only two are obtainable today.

Madame Radek, who last year showed a genius for the making of sandwiches with chopped leeks, and did good work for as head of the Committee for dealing with n war prisoners, came and sat down beside me, and complained bitterly that the authorities wanted to turn her out of the grand ducal apartments in the Kremlin and make them into a historical museum to illustrate the manner of life of the Romanovs. She said she was sure that was simply an excuse and that the real reason was that Madame Trotsky did not like her having a better furnished room than her own. It seems that the Trotskys, when they moved into the Kremlin, chose a lodging extremely modest in comparison with the gorgeous place where I had found Madame Radek.

All this time the room was filling, as the party meeting ended and the members of the Executive Committee came in to take their places. I was asking Litvinov whether he was going to speak, when a little hairy energetic man came up and with great delight showed us the new matches invented in the Soviet laboratories. is short of match−wood, and without paraffin. Besides which I think I am right in saying that the bulk of the matches used in the north came from factories in Finland. In these new Bolshevik matches neither wood nor paraffin is used. Waste paper is a substitute for one, and the grease that is left after cleaning wool is a substitute for the other. The little man, Berg, secretary of the Presidium of the Council of Public Economy, gave me a packet of his matches. They are like the matches in a folding cover that used to be common in Paris. You break off a match before striking it. They strike and burn better than any matches I have ever bought in , and I do not see why they should not be made in England, where we have to import all the materials of which ordinary matches are made. I told Berg I should try to patent them and so turn myself into a capitalist. Another Communist, who was listening, laughed, and said that most fortunes were founded in just such a fraudulent way.

Then there was Steklov of the Izvestia, Madame Kollontai, and a lot of other people whose names I do not remember. Little Bucharin, the editor of Pravda and one of the most interesting talkers in Moscow, who is ready to discuss any philosophy you like, from Berkeley and Locke down to Bergson and William James, trotted up and shook hands. Suddenly a most unexpected figure limped through the door. This was the lame Eliava of the Vologda Soviet, who came up in great surprise at seeing me again, and reminded me how Radek and I, hungry from Moscow, astonished the hotel of the Golden Anchor by eating fifteen eggs apiece, when we came to Vologda last summer (I acted as translator during Radek's conversations with the American Ambassador and Mr. Lindley). Eliava is a fine, honest fellow, and had a very difficult time in Vologda where the large colony of foreign embassies and missions naturally became the centre of disaffection in a district which at the time was full of inflammable material. I remember when we parted from him, Radek said to me that he hardly thought he would see him alive again. He told me he had left Vologda some three months ago and was now going to Turkestan. He did not disguise the resentment he felt towards M. Noulens (the French Ambassador) who, he thought, had stood in the way of agreement last year, but said that he had nothing whatever to say against Lindley.

At last there was a little stir in the raised presidium, and the meeting began. When I saw the lean, long-haired Avanesov take his place as secretary, and Sverdlov, the president, lean forward a little, ring his bell, and announce that the meeting was open and that "Comrade Chicherin has the word," I could hardly believe that I had been away six months.

Chicherin's speech took the form of a general report on the international situation. He spoke a little more clearly than he was used to do, but even so I had to walk round to a place close under the tribune before I could hear him. He sketched the history of the various steps the Soviet Government has taken in trying to secure peace, even including such minor "peace offensives" as Litvinov's personal telegram to President Wilson. He then weighed, in no very hopeful spirit, the possibilities of this last Note to all the Allies having any serious result. He estimated the opposing tendencies for and against war with in each of the principal countries concerned. The growth of revolutionary feeling abroad made imperialistic governments even more aggressive towards the Workers' and Peasants' Republic than they would otherwise be. It was now making their intervention difficult, but no more. It was impossible to say that the collapse of Imperialism had gone so far that it had lost its teeth. Chicherin speaks as if he were a dead man or a ventriloquist's lay figure. And indeed he is half–dead. He has never learnt the art of releasing himself from drudgery by handing it over to his subordinates. He is permanently tired out. You feel it is almost cruel to say "Good morning" to him when you meet him, because of the appeal to be left alone that comes unconsciously into his eyes. Partly in order to avoid people, partly because he is himself accustomed to work at night, his section of the foreign office keeps extraordinary hours, is not to be found till about five in the afternoon and works till four in the morning. The actual material of his report was interesting, but there was nothing in its manner to rouse enthusiasm of any kind. The audience listened with attention, but only woke into real animation when with a shout of laughter it heard an address sent to Cl=82menceau by the emigr=82 financiers, aristocrats and bankrupt politicians of the n colony in Stockholm, protesting against any sort of agreement with the Bolsheviks.

Bucharin followed Chicherin. A little eager figure in his neat brown clothes (bought, I think, while visiting Berlin as a member of the Economic Commission), he at least makes himself clearly heard, though his voice has a funny tendency to breaking. He compared the present situation with the situation before Brest. He had himself (as I well remember) been with Radek, one of the most violent opponents of the Brest peace, and he now admitted that at that time Lenin had been right and he wrong. The position was now different, because whereas then imperialism was split into two camps fighting each other, it now showed signs of uniting its forces. He regarded the League of Nations as a sort of capitalist syndicate, and said that the difference in the French and American attitude towards the League depended upon the position of French and American capital. Capital in France was so weak, that she could at best be only a small shareholder. Capital in America was in a very advantageous position. America therefore wanted a huge All–European syndicate in which each state would have a certain number of shares. America, having the greatest number of shares, would be able to exploit all the other nations. This is a fixed idea of Bucharin's, and he has lost no opportunity of putting out this theory of the League of Nations since the middle of last summer. As for Chicherin's

Note, he said it had at least great historical interest on account of the language it used, which was very different from the hypocritical language of ordinary diplomacy. Here were no phrases about noble motives, but a plain recognition of the facts of the case. "Tell us what you want," it says, "and we are ready to buy you off, in order to avoid armed conflict." Even if the Allies gave no answer the Note would still have served a useful purpose and would be a landmark in history.

Litvinov followed Bucharin. A solid, jolly, round man, with his peaked grey fur hat on his head, rounder than ever in fur–collared, thick coat, his eye–glasses slipping from his nose as he got up, his grey muffler hanging from his neck, he hurried to the tribune. Taking off his things and leaving them on a chair below, he stepped up into the tribune with his hair all rumpled, a look of extreme seriousness on his face, and spoke with a voice whose capacity and strength astonished me who had not heard him speak in public before. He spoke very well, with more sequence than Bucharin, and much vitality, and gave his summary of the position abroad. He said (and Lenin expressed the same view to me afterwards) that the hostility of different countries to Soviet varied in direct proportion to their fear of revolution at home. Thus France, whose capital had suffered most in the war and was weakest, was the most uncompromising, while America, whose capital was in a good position, was ready for agreement. England, with rather less confidence, he thought was ready to follow America. Need of raw material was the motive tending towards agreement with . Fear that the mere existence of a Labour Government anywhere in the world strengthens the revolutionary movement elsewhere, was the motive for the desire to wipe out the Soviet at all cost. Chicherin's note, he thought, would emphasize the difference between these opposing views and would tend to make impossible an alliance of the capitalists against .

Finally, Kamenev, now President of the Moscow Soviet, spoke, objecting to Bucharin's comparison of the peace now sought with that of Brest Litovsk. Then everything was in a state of experiment and untried. Now it was clear to the world that the unity of could be achieved only under the Soviets. The powers opposed to them could not but recognize this fact. Some parts of (Ukraine) had during the last fifteen months experienced every kind of government, from the Soviets, the dictatorship of the proletariat, to the dictatorship of foreign invaders and the dictatorship of a General of the old regime, and they had after all returned to the Soviets. Western European imperialists must realize that the only Government in which rested on the popular masses was the Government of the Soviets and no other. Even the paper of the Mensheviks, commenting on Chicherin's note, had declared that by this step the Soviet Government had shown that it was actually a national Government acting in the interests of the nation. He further read a statement by Right Social Revolutionaries (delegates of that group, members of the Constituent Assembly, were in the gallery) to the effect that they were prepared to help the Soviet Government as the only Government in that was fighting against a dictatorship of the bourgeoisie.

Finally, the Committee unanimously passed a resolution approving every step taken in trying to obtain peace, and at the same time "sending a fraternal greeting to the Red Army of workers and peasants engaged in ensuring the independence of Soviet ." The meeting then turned to talk of other things.

I left, rather miserable to think how little I had foreseen when Soviet was compelled last year to sign an oppressive peace with Germany, that the time would come when they would be trying to buy peace from ourselves. As I went out I saw another unhappy figure, unhappy for quite different reasons. Angelica Balabanova, after dreaming all her life of socialism in the most fervent Utopian spirit, had come at last to to find that a socialist state was faced with difficulties at least as real as those which confront other states, that in the battle there was little sentiment and much cynicism, and that dreams worked out in terms of humanity in the face of the opposition of the whole of the rest of the world are not easily recognized by their dreamers. Poor little Balabanova, less than five feet high, in a black coat that reached to her feet but did not make her look any taller, was wandering about like a lost and dejected spirit. Not so, she was thinking, should socialists deal with their enemies. Somehow, but not so. Had the silver trumpets blown seven times in vain, and was it really necessary to set to work and, stone by stone, with bleeding hands, level the walls of Jericho?

There was snow falling as I walked home. Two workmen, arguing, were walking in front of me. "If only it were not for the hunger," said one. "But will that ever change?" said the other.

KAMENEV AND THE MOSCOW SOVIET

February 11th.

The in 1919

Litvinov has been unlucky in his room in the Metropole. It is small, dark and dirty, and colder than mine. He was feeling ill and his chest was hurting him, perhaps because of his speech last night; but while I was there Kamenev rang him up on the telephone, told him he had a car below, and would he come at once to the Moscow Soviet to speak on the international situation! Litvinov tried to excuse himself, but it was no use, and he said to me that if I wanted to see Kamenev I had better come along. We found Kamenev in the hall, and after a few minutes in a little Ford car we were at the Moscow Soviet. The Soviet meets in the small lecture theatre of the old Polytechnic. When we arrived, a party meeting was going on, and Kamenev, Litvinov, and I went behind the stage to a little empty room, where we were joined by a member of the Soviet whose name I forget.

It was Kamenev's first talk with Litvinov after his return, and I think they forgot that I was there. Kamenev asked Litvinov what he meant to do, and Litvinov told him he wished to establish a special department of control to receive all complaints, to examine into the efficiency of different commissariats, to get rid of parallelism, etc., and, in fact, to be the most unpopular department in Moscow. Kamenev laughed. "You need not think you are the first to have that idea. Every returning envoy without exception has the same. Coming back from abroad they notice more than we do the inefficiencies here, and at once think they will set everything right. Rakovsky sat here for months dreaming of nothing else. Joffe was the same when he came back from that tidy Berlin. Now you; and when Vorovsky comes (Vorovsky was still in Petrograd) I am ready to wager that he too has a scheme for general control waiting in his pocket. The thing cannot be done. The only way is, when something obviously needs doing, to put in some one we can trust to get it done. Soap is hard to get. Good. Establish a commission and soap instantly disappears. But put in one man to see that soap is forthcoming, and somehow or other we get it."

"Where is the soap industry concentrated?"

"There are good factories, well equipped, here, but they are not working, partly for lack of material and partly, perhaps, because some crazy fool imagined that to take an inventory you must bring everything to a standstill."

Litvinov asked him what he thought of the position as a whole. He said good, if only transport could be improved; but before the public of Moscow could feel an appreciable improvement it would be necessary that a hundred wagons of foodstuffs should be coming in daily. At present there are seldom more than twenty. I asked Kamenev about the schools, and he explained that one of their difficulties was due to the militarism forced upon them by external attacks. He explained that the new Red Army soldiers, being mostly workmen, are accustomed to a higher standard of comfort than the old army soldiers, who were mostly peasants. They objected to the planks which served as beds in the old, abominable, over–crowded and unhealthy barracks. Trotsky, looking everywhere for places to put his darlings, found nothing more suitable than the schools; and, in Kamenev's words, "We have to fight hard for every school." Another difficulty, he said, was the lack of school books. Histories, for example, written under the censorship and in accordance with the principles of the old regime, were now useless, and new ones were not ready, apart from the difficulty of getting paper and of printing. A lot, however, was being done. There was no need for a single child in Moscow to go hungry. 150,000 to 180,000 children got free meals daily in the schools. Over 10,000 pairs of felt boots had been given to children who needed them. The number of libraries had enormously increased. Physically workmen lived in far worse conditions than in 1912, but as far as their spiritual welfare was concerned there could be no comparison. Places like the famous Yar restaurant, where once the rich went to amuse themselves with orgies of feeding and drinking and flirting with gypsies, were now made into working men's clubs and theatres, where every working man had a right to go. As for the demand for literature from the provinces, it was far beyond the utmost efforts of the presses and the paper stores to supply.

When the party meeting ended, we went back to the lecture room where the members of the Soviet had already settled themselves in their places. I was struck at once by the absence of the general public which in the old days used to crowd the galleries to overflowing. The political excitement of the revolution has passed, and today there were no more spectators than are usually to be found in the gallery of the House of Commons. The character of the Soviet itself had not changed. Practically every man sitting on the benches was obviously a workman and keenly intent on what was being said. Litvinov practically repeated his speech of last night, making it, however, a little more demagogic in character, pointing out that after the Allied victory, the only corner of the world not dominated by Allied capital was Soviet .

The Soviet passed a resolution expressing "firm confidence that the Soviet Government will succeed in getting peace and so in opening a wide road to the construction of a proletarian state." A note was passed up to Kamenev who, glancing at it, announced that the newly elected representative of the Chinese workmen in Moscow wished to speak. This was Chitaya Kuni, a solid little Chinaman with a big head, in black leather coat and breeches. I had often seen him before, and wondered who he was. He was received with great cordiality and made a quiet, rather shy speech in which he told them he was learning from them how to introduce socialism in China, and more compliments of the same sort. Reinstein replied, telling how at an American labour congress some years back the Americans shut the door in the face of a representative of a union of foreign workmen. "Such," he said, "was the feeling in America at the time when Gompers was supreme, but that time has passed." Still, as I listened to Reinstein, I wondered in how many other countries besides , a representative of foreign labour would be thus welcomed. The reason has probably little to do with the good–heartedness of the ns. Owing to the general unification of wages Mr. Kuni could not represent the competition of cheap labour. I talked to the Chinaman afterwards. He is president of the Chinese Soviet. He told me they had just about a thousand Chinese workmen in Moscow, and therefore had a right to representation in the government of the town. I asked about the Chinese in the Red Army, and he said there were two or three thousand, not more.

AN EX–CAPITALIST

February 13th.

I drank tea with an old acquaintance from the provinces, a n who, before the revolution, owned a leather–bag factory which worked in close connection with his uncle's tannery. He gave me a short history of events at home. The uncle had started with small capital, and during the war had made enough to buy outright the tannery in which he had had shares. The story of his adventures since the October revolution is a very good illustration of the rough and ready way in which theory gets translated into practice. I am writing it, as nearly as possible, as it was told by the nephew.

During the first revolution, that is from March till October 1917, he fought hard against the workmen, and was one of the founders of a Soviet of factory owners, the object of which was to defeat the efforts of the workers' Soviets.* [(*)By agreeing upon lock–outs,etc.] This, of course, was smashed by the October Revolution, and "Uncle, after being forced, as a property owner, to pay considerable contributions, watched the newspapers closely, realized that after the nationalization of the banks resistance was hopeless, and resigned himself to do what he could, not to lose his factory altogether."

He called together all the workmen, and proposed that they should form an artel or co–operative society and take the factory into their own hands, each man contributing a thousand roubles towards the capital with which to run it. Of course the workmen had not got a thousand roubles apiece, "so uncle offered to pay it in for them, on the understanding that they would eventually pay him back." This was illegal, but the little town was a long way from the centre of things, and it seemed a good way out of the difficulty. He did not expect to get it back, but he hoped in this way to keep control of the tannery, which he wished to develop, having a paternal interest in it.

Things worked very well. They elected a committee of control. "Uncle was elected president, I was elected vice–president, and there were three workmen. We are working on those lines to this day. They give uncle 1,500 roubles a month, me a thousand, and the bookkeeper a thousand. The only difficulty is that the men will treat uncle as the owner, and this may mean trouble if things go wrong. Uncle is for ever telling them, It's your factory, don't call me Master,' and they reply, 'Yes, it's our factory all right, but you are still Master, and that must be.'"

Trouble came fast enough, with the tax levied on the propertied classes. "Uncle," very wisely, had ceased to be a property owner. He had given up his house to the factory, and been allotted rooms in it, as president of the factory Soviet. He was therefore really unable to pay when the people from the District Soviet came to tell him that he had been assessed to pay a tax of sixty thousand roubles. He explained the position. The nephew was also present and joined in the argument, whereupon the tax–collectors consulted a bit of paper and retorted, "A tax of twenty thousand has been assessed on you too. Be so good as to put your coat on."

That meant arrest, and the nephew said he had five thousand roubles and would pay that, but could pay no more. Would that do?

"Very well," said the tax–collector, "fetch it."

The nephew fetched it.

"And now put your coat on."

The in 1919

"But you said it would be all right if I paid the five thousand!"

"That's the only way to deal with people like you. We recognize that your case is hard, and we dare say that you will get off. But the Soviet has told us to collect the whole tax or the people who refuse to pay it, and they have decreed that if we came back without one or the other, we shall go to prison ourselves. You can hardly expect us to go and sit in prison out of pity for you. So on with your coat and come along."

They went, and at the militia headquarters were shut into a room with barred windows where they were presently joined by most of the other rich men of the town, all in a rare state of indignation, and some of them very angry with "Uncle," for taking things so quietly. "Uncle was worrying about nothing in the world but the tannery and the leather-works which he was afraid might get into difficulties now that both he and I were under lock and key."

The plutocracy of the town being thus gathered in the little room at the militia-house, their wives came, timorously at first, and chattered through the windows. My informant, being unmarried, sent word to two or three of his friends, in order that he might not be the only one without some one to talk with outside. The noise was something prodigious, and the head of the militia finally ran out into the street and arrested one of the women, but was so discomfited when she removed her shawl and he recognized her as his hostess at a house where he had been billeted as a soldier that he hurriedly let her go. The extraordinary parliament between the rich men of the town and their wives and friends, like a crowd of hoodie crows, chattering outside the window, continued until dark.

Next day the workmen from the tannery came to the militia-house and explained that "Uncle" had really ceased to be a member of the propertied classes, that he was necessary to them as president of their soviet, and that they were willing to secure his release by paying half of the tax demanded from him out of the factory funds. Uncle got together thirty thousand, the factory contributed another thirty, and he was freed, being given a certificate that he had ceased to be an exploiter or a property owner, and would in future be subject only to such taxes as might be levied on the working population. The nephew was also freed, on the grounds that he was wanted at the leather-works.

I asked him how things were going on. He said, "Fairly well, only uncle keeps worrying because the men still call him 'Master.' Otherwise, he is very happy because he has persuaded the workmen to set aside a large proportion of the profits for developing the business and building a new wing to the tannery."

"Do the men work?"

"Well," he said, "we thought that when the factory was in their own hands they would work better, but we do not think they do so, not noticeably, anyhow."

"Do they work worse?"

"No, that is not noticeable either."

I tried to get at his political views. Last summer he had told me that the Soviet Government could not last more than another two or three months. He was then looking forward to its downfall. Now he did not like it any better, but he was very much afraid of war being brought into , or rather of the further disorders which war would cause. He took a queer sort of pride in the way in which the territory of the n republic was gradually resuming its old frontiers. "In the old days no one ever thought the Red Army would come to anything," he said. "You can't expect much from the Government, but it does keep order, and I can do my work and rub along all right." It was quite funny to hear him in one breath grumbling at the revolution and in the next anxiously asking whether I did not think they had weathered the storm, so that there would be no more disorders.

Knowing that in some country places there had been appalling excesses, I asked him how the Red Terror that followed the attempt on the life of Lenin had shown itself in their district. He laughed.

"We got off very cheaply," he said. "This is what happened. A certain rich merchant's widow had a fine house, with enormous stores of all kinds of things, fine knives and forks, and too many of everything. For instance, she had twenty-two samovars of all sizes and sorts. Typical merchant's house, so many tablecloths that they could not use them all if they lived to be a hundred. Well, one fine day, early last summer, she was told that her house was wanted and that she must clear out. For two days she ran hither and thither trying to get out of giving it up. Then she saw it was no good, and piled all those things, samovars and knives and forks and dinner services and tablecloths and overcoats (there were over a dozen fur overcoats) in the garrets which she closed and sealed, and got the president of the Soviet to come and put his seal also. In the end things were so friendly that he even put a sentinel there to see that the seal should not be broken. Then came the news from Petrograd and Moscow about the Red terror, and the Soviet, after holding a meeting and deciding that it ought to do something, and being on too good terms with all of us to do anything very bad, suddenly remembered poor Maria Nicolaevna's garrets. They broke the seals and tumbled out all the kitchen things, knives, forks, plates, furniture, the twenty–two samovars and the overcoats, took them in carts to the Soviet and declared them national property. National property! And a week or two later there was a wedding of a daughter of one of the members of the Soviet, and somehow or other the knives and forks were on the table, and as for samovars, there were enough to make tea for a hundreds."

A THEORIST OF REVOLUTION

February 13th.

After yesterday's talk with a capitalist victim of the revolution, I am glad for the sake of contrast to set beside it a talk with one of the revolution's chief theorists. The leather–worker illustrated the revolution as it affects an individual. The revolutionary theorist was quite incapable of even considering his own or any other individual interests and thought only in terms of enormous movements in which the experiences of an individual had only the significance of the adventures of one ant among a myriad. Bucharin, member of the old economic mission to Berlin, violent opponent of the Brest peace, editor of Pravda, author of many books on economics and revolution, indefatigable theorist, found me drinking tea at a table in the Metropole.

I had just bought a copy of a magazine which contained a map of the world, in which most of Europe was coloured red or pink for actual or potential revolution. I showed it to Bucharin and said, "You cannot be surprised that people abroad talk of you as of the new Imperialists."

Bucharin took the map and looked at it.

"Idiotism, rank idiotism!" he said. "At the same time," he added, "I do think we have entered upon a period of revolution which may last fifty years before the revolution is at last victorious in all Europe and finally in all the world."

Now, I have a stock theory which I am used to set before revolutionaries of all kinds, nearly always with interesting results. (See p.118.) I tried it on Bucharin. I said:–

"You people are always saying that there will be revolution in England. Has it not occurred to you that England is a factory and not a granary, so that in the event of revolution we should be immediately cut off from all food supplies. According to your own theories, English capital would unite with American in ensuring that within six weeks the revolution had nothing to eat. England is not a country like where you can feed yourselves somehow or other by simply walking to where there is food. Six weeks would see starvation and reaction in England. I am inclined to think that a revolution in England would do more harm than good."

Bucharin laughed. "You old counter–revolutionary!" he said. "That would be all true, but you must look further. You are right in one thing. If the revolution spreads in Europe, America will cut off food supplies. But by that time we shall be getting food from Siberia."

"And is the poor Siberian railway to feed , Germany, and England?"

"Before then Pichon and his friends will have gone. There will be France to feed too. But you must not forget that there are the cornfields of Hungary and Roumania. Once civil war ends in Europe, Europe can feed herself. With English and German engineering assistance we shall soon turn into an effective grain supply for all the working men's republics of the Continent. But even then the task will be only beginning. The moment there is revolution in England, the English colonies will throw themselves eagerly into the arms of America. Then will come America's turn, and, finally, it is quite likely that we shall all have to combine to overthrow the last stronghold of capitalism in some South African bourgeois republic. I can well imagine," he said, looking far away with his bright little eyes through the walls of the dark dining room, "that the working men's republics of Europe may have to have a colonial policy of an inverse kind. Just as now you conquer backward races in order to exploit them, so in the future you may have to conquer the colonists to take from them the means of exploitation. There is only one thing I am afraid of."

"And what is that?"

"Sometimes I am afraid that the struggle will be so bitter and so long drawn out that the whole of European culture may be trampled under foot."

I thought of my leather–worker of yesterday, one of thousands experiencing in their own persons the appalling discomforts, the turn over and revaluation of all established values that revolution, even without death and civil war, means to the ordinary man; and, being perhaps a little faint–hearted, I finished my tea in silence. Bucharin, after carelessly opening these colossal perspectives, drank his tea in one gulp, prodigiously sweetened with my saccharin, reminded me of his illness in the summer, when Radek scoured the town for sweets for him, curing him with no other medicine, and then hurried off, fastening his coat as he went, a queer little De Quincey of revolution, to disappear into the dusk, before, half running, half walking, as his way is, he reached the other end of the big dimly lit, smoke–filled dining room.

EFFECTS OF ISOLATION

February 14th.

I had a rather grim talk with Meshtcheriakov at dinner. He is an old Siberian exile, who visited England last summer. He is editing a monthly magazine in Moscow, mostly concerned with the problems of reconstrucition, and besides that doing a lot of educational work among the labouring classes. He is horrified at the economic position of the country. Isolation, he thinks, is forcing backwards towards a primeval state.

"We simply cannot get things. For example, I am lecturing on Mathematics. I have more pupils than I can deal with. They are as greedy for knowledge as sponges for water, and I cannot get even the simplest text–books for them. I cannot even find in the second–hand book stores an old Course of Mathematics from which I could myself make a series of copies for them. I have to teach like a teacher of the middle ages. But, like him, I have pupils who want to learn."

"In another three years," said some one else at the table, "we shall be living in ruins. Houses in Moscow were always kept well warmed. Lack of transport has brought with it lack of fuel, and water–pipes have burst in thousands of houses. We cannot get what is needed to mend them. In the same way we cannot get paints for the walls, which are accordingly rotting. In another three years we shall have all the buildings of Moscow tumbling about our ears."

Some one else joined in with a laugh: "In ten years we shall be running about on all fours."

"And in twenty we shall begin sprouting tails."

Meshtcheriakov finished his soup and laid down his wooden spoon.

"There is another side to all these things," he said. "In , even if the blockade lasts, we shall get things established again sooner than anywhere else, because we have all the raw materials in our own country. With us it is a question of transport only, and of transport within our own borders. In a few years, I am convinced, in spite of all that is working against us, will be a better place to live in than anywhere else in Europe. But we have a bad time to go through. And not we alone. The effects of the war are scarcely visible as yet in the west, but they will become visible. Humanity has a period of torment before it . . . ."

"Bucharin says fifty years," I said, referring to my talk of yesterday.

"Maybe. I think less than that. But the revolution will be far worse for you nations of the west than it has been for us. In the west, if there is revolution, they will use artillery at once, and wipe out whole districts. The governing classes in the west are determined and organized in a way our home–grown capitalists never were. The Autocracy never allowed them to organize, so, when the Autocracy itself fell, our task was comparatively easy. There was nothing in the way. It will not be like that in Germany."

AN EVENING AT THE OPERA

I read in one of the newspapers that a member of the American Commission in Berlin reasoned from the fact that the Germans were crowding to theatres and spectacles that they could not be hungry. There can be no question about the hunger of the people of

Moscow, but the theatres are crowded, and there is such demand for seats that speculators acquire tickets in the legitimate way and sell them illicitly near the doors of the theatre to people who have not been able to get in, charging, of course, double the price or even more. Interest in the theatre, always keen in Moscow, seems to me to have rather increased than decreased. There is a School of Theatrical Production, with lectures on every subject connected with the stage, from stage carpentry upwards. A Theatrical Bulletin is published three times weekly, containing the programmes of all the theatres and occasional articles on theatrical subjects. I had been told in Stockholm that the Moscow theatres were closed. The following is an incomplete list of the plays and spectacles to be seen at various theatres on February 13 and February 14, copied from the Theatrical Bulletin of those dates. Just as it would be interesting to know what French audiences enjoyed at the time of the French revolution, so I think it worth while to record the character of the entertainments at present popular in Moscow.

Opera at the Great Theatre.—"Sadko" by Rimsky–Korsakov and "Samson and Delilah" by Saint–Saens.

Small State Theatre.—"Besheny Dengi" by Ostrovsky and "Starik" by Gorky.

Moscow Art Theatre.— "The Cricket on the Hearth" by Dickens and "The Death of Pazuchin" by Saltykov–Shtchedrin.

Opera. "Selo Stepantchiko" and "Coppellia."

People's Palace.—"Dubrovsky" by Napravnik and "Demon" by Rubinstein.

Zamoskvoretzky Theatre.—"Groza" by Ostrovsky and "Meshitchane" by Gorky.

Popular Theatre.—" The Miracle of Saint, Anthony" by Maeterlinck.

Komissarzhevskaya Theatre.—"A Christmas Carol" by Dickens and "The Accursed Prince" by Remizov.

Korsh Theatre.—"Much Ado about Nothing" by Shakespeare and "Le Misanthrope" and "Georges Dandin" by Moli=8Are.

The in 1919

Dramatic Theatre.—"Alexander I" by Merezhkovsky.

Theatre of Drama and Comedy.— "Little Dorrit" by Dickens and "The King's Barber" by Lunacharsky.

Besides these, other theatres were playing K. R. (Konstantin Romanov), Ostrovsky, Potapenko, Vinitchenko, etc. The two Studios of the Moscow Art Theatre were playing "Rosmersholm" and a repertoire of short plays. They, like the Art Theatre Company, occasionally play in the suburban theatres when their place at home is taken by other performers.

I went to the Great State Theatre to Saint–Saens' "Samson and Delilah." I had a seat in the box close above the orchestra, from which I could obtain a view equally good of the stage and of the house. Indeed, the view was rather better of the house than of the stage. But that was as I had wished, for the house was what I had come to see.

It had certainly changed greatly since the pre–revolutionary period. The Moscow plutocracy of bald merchants and bejewelled fat wives had gone. Gone with them were evening dresses and white shirt fronts. The whole audience was in the monotone of everyday clothes. The only contrast was given by a small group of Tartar women in the dress circle, who were shawled in white over head and shoulders, in the Tartar fashion. There were many soldiers, and numbers of men who had obviously come straight from their work. There were a good many grey and brown woollen jerseys about, and people were sitting in overcoats of all kinds and ages, for the theatre was very cold. (This, of course, was due to lack of fuel, which may in the long run lead to a temporary stoppage of the theatres if electricity cannot be spared for lighting them.) The orchestra was also variously dressed. Most of the players of brass instruments had evidently been in regimental bands during the war, and still retained their khaki–green tunics with a very mixed collection of trousers and breeches. Others were in every kind of everyday clothes. The conductor alone wore a frock coat, and sat in his place like a specimen from another age, isolated in fact by his smartness alike from his ragged orchestra and from the stalls behind him.

I looked carefully to see the sort of people who fill the stalls under the new regime, and decided that there has been a general transfer of brains from the gallery to the floor of the house. The same people who in the old days scraped kopecks and waited to get a good place near the ceiling now sat where formerly were the people who came here to digest their dinners. Looking from face to face that night I thought there were very few people in the theatre who had had anything like a good dinner to digest. But, as for their keenness, I can imagine few audiences to which, from the actor's point of view, it would be better worth while to play. Applause, like brains, had come down from the galleries.

Of the actual performance I have little to say except that ragged clothes and empty stomachs seemed to make very little difference to the orchestra. Helzer, the ballerina, danced as well before this audience as ever before the bourgeoisie. As I turned up the collar of my coat I reflected that the actors deserved all the applause they got for their heroism in playing in such cold. Now and then during the evening I was unusually conscious of the unreality of opera generally, perhaps because of the contrast in magnificence between the stage and the shabby, intelligent audience. Now and then, on the other hand, stage and audience seemed one and indivisible. For "Samson and Delilah" is itself a poem of revolution, and gained enormously by being played by people every one of whom had seen something of the sort in real life. Samson's stirring up of the Israelites reminded me of many scenes in Petrograd in 1917, and when, at last, he brings the temple down in ruins on his triumphant enemies, I was reminded of the words attributed to Trotsky:– "If we are, in the end, forced to go, we shall slam the door behind us in such away that the echo shall be felt throughout the world."

Going home afterwards through the snow, I did not see a single armed man. A year ago the streets were deserted after ten in the evening except by those who, like myself, had work which took them to meetings and such things late at night. They used to be empty except for the military pickets round their log–fires. Now they were full of foot–passengers going home from the theatres, utterly forgetful of the fact that only twelve months before they had thought the streets of Moscow unsafe after dark. There could be no question about it. The revolution is settling down, and people now think of other matters than the old question, will it last one week or two?

THE COMMITTEE OF STATE CONSTRUCTIONS

February 15th.

I went by appointment to see Pavlovitch, President of the Committee of State

Constructions. It was a very jolly morning and the streets were crowded. As I walked through the gate into the Red Square I saw the usual crowd of peasant women at the little chapel of the Iberian Virgin, where there was a blaze of candles. On the wall of what used, I think, to be the old town hall, close by the gate, some fanatic agnostic has set a white inscription on a tablet, "Religion is opium for the People." The tablet, which has been there a long time, is in shape not unlike the customary frame for a sacred picture. I saw an old peasant, evidently unable to read, cross himself solemnly before the chapel, and then, turning to the left, cross himself as solemnly before this anti–religious inscription. It is perhaps worth while to remark in passing that the new Communist programme, while insisting, as before, on the definite separation of church and state, and church and school, now includes the particular statement that "care should be taken in no way to hurt the feelings of the religious." Churches and chapels are open, church processions take place as before, and Moscow, as in the old days, is still a city of church bells.

A long line of sledges with welcome bags of flour was passing through the square. Soldiers of the Red Army were coming off parade, laughing and talking, and very noticeably smarter than the men of six months ago. There was a bright clear sky behind the fantastic Cathedral of St. Basil, and the rough graves under the Kremlin wall, where those are buried who died in the fighting at the time of the November Revolution, have been tidied up. There was scaffolding round the gate of the Kremlin which was damaged at that time and is being carefully repaired.

The Committee of State Constructions was founded last spring to coordinate the management of the various engineering and other constructive works previously carried on by independent departments. It became an independent organ with its own finances about the middle of the summer. Its headquarters are in the Nikolskaya, in the Chinese town, next door to the old building of the Anglo–n Trading Company, which still bears the Lion and the Unicorn sculptured above its green and white fa=87ade some time early in the seventeenth century.

Pavlovitch is a little, fat, spectacled man with a bald head, fringed with the remains of red hair, and a little reddish beard. He was dressed in a black leather coat and trousers. He complained bitterly that all his plans for engineering works to improve the productive possibilities of the country were made impracticable by the imperious demands of war. As an old Siberian exile he had been living in France before the revolution and, as he said, had seen there how France made war. "They sent her locomotives, and rails for the locomotives to run on, everything she needed they sent her from all parts of the world. When they sent horses, they sent also hay for their food, and shoes for their feet, and even nails for the shoes. If we were supplied like that, would be at peace in a week. But we have nothing, and can get nothing, and are forced to be at war against our will.

"And war spoils everything," he continued. "This committee should be at work on affairs of peace, making more useful to herself and to the rest of the world. You know our plans. But with fighting on all our fronts, and with all our best men away, we are compelled to use ninety per cent. of our energy and material for the immediate needs of the army. Every day we get masses of telegrams from all fronts, asking for this or that. For example, Trotsky telegraphs here simply "We shall be in Orenburg in two days," leaving us to do what is necessary. Then with the map before me, I have to send what will be needed, no matter what useful work has to be abandoned meanwhile, engineers, railway gangs for putting right the railways, material for bridges, and so on.

"Indeed, the biggest piece of civil engineering done in for many years was the direct result of our fear lest you people or the Germans should take our Baltic fleet. Save the dreadnoughts we could not, but I decided to save what we could. The widening and deepening of the canal system so as to shift boats from the Baltic to the Volga had been considered in the time of the Tzar. It was considered and dismissed as impracticable. Once, indeed, they did try to take two torpedo–boats over, and they lifted them on barges to make the attempt. Well, we said that as the thing could be planned, it could be done, and the canals are deepened and widened, and we took through them, under their own power, seven big destroyers, six small destroyers and four submarine boats, which, arriving unexpectedly before Kazan, played a great part in our victory there. But the pleasure of that was spoilt for me by the knowledge that I had had to take men and material from the building of the electric power station, with which we hope to make Petrograd independent of the coal supply.

"The difficulties we have to fight against are, of course, enormous, but much of what the old regime failed to do, for want of initiative or for other reasons, we have done and are doing. Some of the difficulties are of a most unexpected kind. The local inhabitants, partly, no doubt, under the influence of our political opponents, were extremely hostile with regard to the building of the power station, simply because they did not understand it. I went there myself, and explained to them what it would mean, that their river would become a rich river, that they would be able to get cheap power for all sorts of works, and that they would have electric light in all their houses. Then they carried me shoulder high through the village, and sent telegrams to Lenin, to Zinoviev, to everybody they could think of, and since then we have had nothing but help from them.

"Most of our energy at present has to be spent on mending and making railways and roads for the use of the army. Over 11,000 versts of railway are under construction, and we have finished the railway from Arzamas to Shikhran. Twelve hundred versts of highroad are under construction. And to meet the immediate needs of the army we have already repaired or made 8,000 versts of roads of various kinds. As a matter of fact the internal railway net of is by no means as bad as people make out. By its means, hampered as we are, we have been able to beat the counter–revolutionaries, concentrating our best troops, now here, now there, wherever need may be. Remember that the whole way round our enormous frontiers we are being forced to fight groups of reactionaries supported at first mostly by the Germans, now mostly by yourselves, by the Roumanians, by the Poles, and in some districts by the Germans still. Troops fighting on the Ural front are fighting a month later south of Voronezh, and a month later again are having a holiday, marching on the heels of the Germans as they evacuate the occupied provinces. Some of our troops are not yet much good. One day they fight, and the next they think they would rather not. So that our best troops, those in which there are most workmen, have to be flung in all directions. We are at work all the time enabling this to be done, and making new roads to enable it to be done still better. But what waste, when there are so many other things we want to do!

"All the time the needs of war are pressing on us. To–day is the first day for two months that we have been able to warm this building. We have been working here in overcoats and fur hats in a temperature below freezing point. Why? Wood was already on its way to us, when we had suddenly to throw troops northwards. Our wood had to be flung out of the wagons, and the Red Army put in its place, and the wagons sent north again. The thing had to be done, and we have had to work as best we could in the cold. Many of my assistants have fallen ill. Two only yesterday had to be taken home in a condition something like that of a fit, the result of prolonged sedentary work in unheated rooms. I have lost the use of my right hand for the same reason." He stretched out his right hand, which he had been keeping in the pocket of his coat. It was an ugly sight, with swollen, immovable fingers, like the roots of a vegetable.

The in 1919

At this moment some one came in to speak to Pavlovitch. He stood at the table a little behind me, so that I did not see him, but Pavlovitch, noticing that he looked curiously at me, said, "Are you acquaintances?" I looked round and saw Sukhanov, Gorky's friend, formerly one of the cleverest writers on the Novaya Jizn. I jumped up and shook hands with him.

"What, have you gone over to the Bolsheviks?" I asked.

"Not at all," said Sukhanov, smiling, "but I am working here."

"Sukhanov thinks that we do less harm than anybody else," said Pavlovitch, and laughed. "Go and talk to him and he'll tell you all there is to be said against us. And there's lots to say."

Sukhanov was an extremely bitter enemy of the Bolsheviks, and was very angry with me when, over a year ago, I told him I was convinced that sooner or later he would be working with them. I told Pavlovitch the story, and he laughed again. "A long time ago," he said, "Sukhanov made overtures to me through Miliutin. I agreed, and everything was settled, but when a note appeared in Pravda to say that he was going to work in this Committee, he grew shy, and wrote a contradiction. Miliutin was very angry and asked me to publish the truth. I refused, but wrote on that day in my diary, Sukhanov will come. Three months later he was already working with us. One day he told me that in the big diary of the revolution which he is writing, and will write very well, he had some special abuse for me. 'I have none for you,' I said, 'but I will show you one page of my own diary,' and I showed him that page, and asked him to look at the date. Sukhanov is an honest fellow, and was bound to come."

He went on with his talk.

"You know, hampered as we are by lack of everything, we could not put up the fight we are putting up against the reactionaries if it were not for the real revolutionary spirit of the people as a whole. The reactionaries have money, munitions, supplies of all kinds, instructors, from outside. We have nothing, and yet we beat them. Do you know that the English have given them tanks? Have you heard that in one place they used gases or something of the kind, and blinded eight hundred men? And yet we win. Why? Because from every town we capture we get new strength. And any town they take is a source of weakness to them, one more town to garrison and hold against the wishes of the population."

"And if you do get peace, what then!"

"We want from abroad all that we cannot make ourselves. We want a hundred thousand versts of rails. Now we have to take up rails in one place to lay them in another. We want new railways built. We want dredgers for our canals and river works. We want excavators."

"And how do you expect people to sell you these things when your foreign credit is not worth a farthing?"

"We shall pay in concessions, giving foreigners the right to take raw materials. Timber, actual timber, is as good as credit. We have huge areas of forest in the north, and every country in Europe needs timber. Let that be our currency for foreign purchases. We are prepared to say, 'You build this, or give us that, and we will give you the right to take so much timber for yourselves.' And so on. And concessions of other kinds also. As a matter of fact negotiations are now proceeding with a foreign firm for the building of a railway from the Obi to Kotlas."

"But part of that district is not in your hands.

"If we get peace we shall be able to arrange that without difficulty."

Just as I was going he stopped me, and evidently not in the least realizing that English people generally have come to think of him and his friends as of some strange sort of devils, if not with horns and tails, certainly far removed from human beings, he asked:—

"If we do get peace, don't you think there will be engineers and skilled labourers in England who will volunteer to come out to and help us? There is so much to do that I can promise they will have the best we can give them. We are almost as short of skilled men as we are of locomotives. We are now taking simple unskilled workmen who show any signs of brains and training them as we go along. There must be engineers, railwaymen, mechanics among English socialists who would be glad to come. And of course they need not be socialists, so long as they are good engineers."

46

That last suggestion of his is entirely characteristic. It is impossible to make the Bolsheviks realize that the English people feel any hostility towards them. Nor do they feel hostility towards the English as such. On my way back to the hotel I met a party of English soldiers, taken prisoners on the northern front, walking free, without a convoy, through the streets.

THE EXECUTIVE COMMITTEE AND THE TERROR

February 17th.

My general impression that the Soviet revolution has passed through its period of internal struggle and is concentrating upon constructive work so far as that is allowed by war on all its frontiers, and that the population is settling down under the new regime, was confirmed by the meeting of the Executive Committee which definitely limited the powers of the Extraordinary Commission. Before the sitting was opened I had a few words with Peters and with Krylenko. The excitement of the internal struggle was over. It had been bitterly fought within the party, and both Krylenko of the Revolutionary Tribunal and Peters of the Extraordinary Commission were there merely to witness the official act that would define their new position. Peters talked of his failure to get away for some shooting; Krylenko jeered at me for having refused to believe in the Lockhart conspiracy. Neither showed any traces of the bitter struggle waged within the party for and against the almost dictatorial powers of the Extraordinary Commission for dealing with counter–revolution.

The sitting opened with a report by Dserzhinsky, that strange ascetic who, when in prison in Warsaw, insisted on doing the dirty work of emptying the slops and cleaning other people's cells besides his own, on a theory that one man should where possible take upon himself the evil which would otherwise have to be shared by all; and in the dangerous beginning of the revolution had taken upon himself the most unpopular of all posts, that of President of the Extraordinary Commission. His personal uprightness is the complement of an absolute personal courage, shown again and again during the last eighteen months. At the time of the Left Social Revolutionary mutiny he went without a guard to the headquarters of the mutineers, believing that he could bring them to reason, and when arrested by them dared them to shoot him and showed so bold a front that in the end the soldiers set to watch him set him free and returned to their allegiance. This thin, tallish man, with a fanatic face not unlike some of the traditional portraits of St. Francis, the terror of counter–revolutionaries and criminals alike, is a very bad speaker. He looks into the air over the heads of his audience and talks as if he were not addressing them at all but some one else unseen. He talks even of a subject which he knows perfectly with curious inability to form his sentences; stops, changes words, and often, recognizing that he cannot finish his sentence, ends where he is, in the middle of it, with a little odd, deprecating emphasis, as if to say: "At this point there is a full stop. At least so it seems."

He gave a short colourless sketch of the history of the Extraordinary Commission. He referred to the various crises with which it had had to deal, beginning with the drunken pogroms in Petrograd, the suppression of the combined anarchists and criminals in Moscow (he mentioned that after that four hours' struggle which ended in the clearing out of the anarchists' strongholds, criminality in Moscow decreased by 80 per cent.), to the days of the Terror when, now here, now there, armed risings against the Soviet were engineered by foreigners and by counter–revolutionaries working with them. He then made the point that throughout all this time the revolution had been threatened by large–scale revolts. Now the revolution was safe from such things and was threatened only by individual treacheries of various kinds, not by things which needed action on a large scale. They had traitors, no doubt, in the Soviet institutions who were waiting for the day (which would never come) to join with their enemies, and meanwhile were secretly hampering their work. They did not need on that account to destroy their institutions as a whole. The struggle with counter–revolution had passed to a new stage. They no longer had to do open battle with open enemies; they had merely to guard themselves against individuals. The laws of war by which, meeting him on the field of battle, the soldier had a right to kill his enemy without trial, no longer held good. The situation was now that of peace, where each offender must have his guilt proved before a court. Therefore the right of sentencing was removed from the Extraordinary Commission; but if, through unforeseen circumstances, the old conditions should return, they intended that the dictatorial powers of the Commission should be restored to it until those conditions had ceased. Thus if, in case of armed counter–revolution, a district were declared to be in a state of war, the Extraordinary Commission would resume its old powers. Otherwise its business would be to hand offenders, such as Soviet officials who were habitually late (here there was a laugh, the only sign throughout his speech that Dserzhinsky was holding the attention of his audience), over to the Revolutionary Tribunal, which would try them and, should their guilt be proved, put them in concentration camps to learn to work. He read point by point the resolutions establishing these, changes and providing for the formation of Revolutionary Tribunals. Trial to take place within forty–eight hours after the conclusion of the investigation, and the investigation to take not longer than a month. He ended as he ended his sentences, as if by accident, and people scarcely realized he had finished before Sverdlov announced the next speaker.

Krylenko proposed an amendment to ensure that no member of the Revolutionary Tribunal could be also a member of the Extraordinary Commission which had taken up and investigated a case. His speech was very disappointing. He is not at his best when addressing a serious meeting like that of the Executive Committee. The Krylenko who spoke to–night, fluently, clearly, but without particular art, is a very different Krylenko from the virtuoso in mob oratory, the little, dangerous, elderly man in ensign's uniform who swayed the soldiers' mass meetings in Petrograd a year and a half ago. I remember hearing him speak in barracks soon after the murder of Shingarev and Kokoshkin, urging class struggle and at the same time explaining the difference between that and the murder of sick men in bed. He referred to the murder and, while continuing his speech, talking already of another subject, be went through the actions of a man approaching a bed and killing a sleeper with a pistol. It was a trick, of course, but the thrilling, horrible effect of it moved the whole audience with a shudder of disgust. There was nothing of this kind in his short lecture on jurisprudence to–night.

Avanesov, the tall, dark secretary of the Executive Committee, with the face of a big, benevolent hawk hooded in long black hair, opposed Krylenko on the ground that there were not enough trustworthy workers to ensure that in country districts such a provision could be carried out. Finally the resolution was passed as a whole and the amendment was referred to the judgment of the presidium.

The Committee next passed to the consideration of the Extraordinary Tax levied on the propertied classes. Krestinsky, Commissary of Finance, made his report to a grim audience, many of whom quite frankly regarded the tax as a political mistake. Krestinsky is a short, humorous man, in dark spectacles, dressed more like a banker than like a Bolshevik. It was clear that the collection of the tax had not been as successful as he had previously suggested. I was interested in his reference to the double purpose of the tax and in the reasons he gave for its comparative failure. The tax had a fiscal purpose, partly to cover deficit, partly by drawing in paper money to raise the value of the rouble. It had also a political purpose. It was intended to affect the propertied classes only, and thus to

49

weaken the Kulaks (hard–fists, rich peasants) in the villages and to teach the poorer peasants the meaning of the revolution. Unfortunately some Soviets, where the minority of the Kulaks had retained the unfair domination given it by its economic strength, had distributed the tax–paying equally over the whole population, thus very naturally raising the resentment of the poor who found themselves taxed to the same amount as those who could afford to pay. It had been necessary to send circular telegrams emphasizing the terms of the decree. In cases where the taxation had been carried out as intended there had been no difficulty. The most significant reason for the partial unsuccess was that the propertied class, as such, had already diminished to a greater extent than had been supposed, and many of those taxed, for example, as factory owners were already working, not as factory owners, but as paid directors in nationalized factories, and were therefore no longer subject to the tax. In other words, the partial failure of the tax was a proof of the successful development of the revolution. (This is illustrated by the concrete case of "Uncle" recorded on p. 73.) Krestinsky believed that the revolution had gone so far that no further tax of , this kind would be either possible or necessary.

NOTES OF CONVERSATIONS WITH LENIN

Whatever else they may think of him, not even his enemies deny that Vladimir Ilyitch Oulianov (Lenin) is one of the greatest personalities of his time. I therefore make no apology for writing down such scraps of his conversation as seem to illustrate his manner of mind.

He was talking of the lack of thinkers in the English labour movement, and said he remembered hearing Shaw speak at some meeting. Shaw, he said, was "A good man fallen among Fabians" and a great deal further left than his company. He had not heard of "The Perfect Wagnerite," but was interested when I told him the general idea of the book, and turned fiercely on an interrupter who said that Shaw was a clown. "He may be a clown for the bourgeoisie in a bourgeois state, but they would not think him a clown in a revolution."

He asked whether Sidney Webb was consciously working in the interests of the capitalists, and when I said I was quite sure that he was not, he said, "Then he has more industry than brains. He certainly has great knowledge."

He was entirely convinced that England was on the eve of revolution, and pooh–poohed my objections. "Three months ago I thought it would end in all the world having to fight the centre of reaction in England. But I do not think so now. Things have gone further there than in France, if the news as to the extent of the strikes is true."

I pointed out some of the circumstances, geographical and economical, which would make the success of a violent revolution in England problematical in the extreme, and put to him the same suggestion that I put to Bucharin (see page 81), namely, that a suppressed movement in England would be worse for than our traditional method of compromise. He agreed at once, but said, "That is quite true, but you cannot stop a revolution . . . although Ramsay MacDonald will try to at the last minute. Strikes and Soviets. If these two habits once get hold, nothing will keep the workmen from them. And Soviets, once started, must sooner or later come to supreme power." Then, "But certainly it would be much more difficult in England. Your big clerk and shop–keeping class would oppose it, until the workmen broke them. was indeed the only country in which the revolution could start. And we are not yet through our troubles with the peasantry."

I suggested that one reason why it had been possible in was that they had had room to retreat.

"Yes," he said. "The distances saved us. The Germans were frightened of them, at the time when they could indeed have eaten us up, and won peace, which the Allies would have given them in gratitude for our destruction. A revolution in England would have nowhere whither to retire."

Of the Soviets he said, "In the beginning I thought they were and would remain a purely n form; but it is now quite clear that under various names they must be the instruments of revolution everywhere."

He expressed the opinion that in England they would not allow me to tell the truth about , and gave as an example the way in which Colonel Robins had been kept silent in America. He asked about Robins, "Had he really been as friendly to the Soviet Government as he made out?" I said, "Yes, if only as a sportsman admiring its pluck and courage in difficulties." I quoted Robins' saying, "I can't go against a baby I have sat up with for six months. But if there were a Bolshevik movement in America I'd be out with my rifle to fight it every time." "Now that," said Lenin, "is an honest man and more far–seeing than most. I always liked that man." He shook with laughter at the image of the baby, and said, "That baby had several million other folk sitting up with it too."

He said he had read in an English socialist paper a comparison of his own theories with those of an American, Daniel De Leon. He had then borrowed some of De Leon's pamphlets from Reinstein (who belongs to the party which De Leon founded in America), read them for the first time, and was amazed to see how far and how early De Leon had pursued the same train of thought as the ns. His theory that representation should be by industries, not by areas, was already the germ of the Soviet system. He remembered seeing De Leon at an International Conference. De Leon made no impression at all, a grey old man, quite unable to speak to such an audience: but evidently a much bigger man than he looked, since his pamphlets were written before the experience of the n Revolution of 1905. Some days afterwards I noticed that Lenin had introduced a few phrases of De Leon, as if to do honour to his memory, into the draft for the new programme of the Communist party.

Talking of the lies that are told about , he said it was interesting to notice that they were mostly perversions of truth and not pure inventions, and gave as an example the recent story that he had recanted. "Do you know the origin of that?" he said. "I was wishing a happy New Year to a friend over the telephone, and said 'And may we commit fewer stupidities this year than last!' Some one overheard it and told some one else. A newspaper announced Lenin says we are committing stupidities' and so the story started."

More than ever, Lenin struck me as a happy man. Walking home from the Kremlin, I tried to think of any other man of his calibre who had had a similar joyous temperament. I could think of none. This little, bald–headed, wrinkled man, who tilts his chair this way and that, laughing over one thing or another, ready any minute to give serious advice to any who interrupt him to ask for it, advice so well reasoned that it is to his followers far more compelling than any command, every one of his wrinkles is a wrinkle of laughter, not of worry. I think the reason must be that he is the first great leader who utterly discounts the value of his own personality. He is quite without personal ambition. More than that, he believes, as a Marxist, in the movement of the masses which, with or without him, would still move. His whole faith is in the elemental forces that move people, his faith in himself is merely his belief that be justly estimates the direction of those forces. He does not believe that any man could make or stop the revolution which he thinks inevitable. If the n revolution fails, according to him, it fails only temporarily, and because of forces beyond any man's control. He is consequently free with a freedom no other great man has ever had. It is not so much what he says that inspires confidence in him. It is this sensible freedom, this obvious detachment. With his philosophy he cannot for a moment believe that one man's mistake might ruin all. He is, for himself at any rate, the exponent, not the cause, of the events that will be for ever linked with his name.

THE SUPREME COUNCIL OF PUBLIC ECONOMY

February 20th.

To—day was an unlucky day. I felt tired, ill and hungry, and had arranged to talk with both Rykov, the President of the Supreme Council of People's Economy, and Krestinsky, the Commissar of Finance, at such awkward times that I got no tea and could get nothing to eat until after four o'clock. Two such talks on an empty stomach (for the day before I had had only a plate of soup and a little scrap of fish) were a little too much for me, and I fear I did not gather as much information as I should have collected under better conditions.

I had a jolly drive, early in the morning, through the Chinese Town, and out by the gate in the old wall, up Myasnitzkaya Street, and round to the right to a building that used to be the Grand Hotel of Siberia, a loathsome place where I once stayed. Here in the old days provincial merchants put up, who did not mind high prices and a superfluity of bugs. It has now been turned into a hive of office work, and is the headquarters of the Supreme Council of Public Economy, which, controlling production and distribution alike, is the centre of the constructive work going on throughout the country.

This Council, the theorists tell me, is intended to become the central organization of the state. The Soviets will naturally become less and less important as instruments of political transition as that transition is completed and the struggle against reaction within and without comes to an end. Then the chief business of the state will no longer be to protect itself against enemies but to develop its economic life, to increase its productivity and to improve the material conditions of the workers of whom it is composed. All these tasks are those of the Supreme Council of Public Economy, and as the bitterness of the struggle dies away this body, which came into being almost unnoticed in the din of battle, will become more and more important in comparison with the Soviets, which were in origin not constructive organizations but the instruments of a revolution, the hardest stages of which have already been accomplished.

It is perhaps worth while to set out here the constitution of this Council. It is considered at present as the economic department of the All–n Central Executive Committee, to which, and to the Council of People's Commissaries, it is responsible. It regulates all production and distribution. It reports on the various estimates of the state budget and, in conjunction with the Commissariats of Finance and State Control, carries out the financing of all branches of public economy. It consists of 69 members, and is composed as follows:—Ten representatives from the All–n Executive Committee, thirty from the All–n Industrial Productive Union (a union of Trade Unions), twenty from the ten District Councils of Public Economy, two from the All–n Council of Workers' Cooperative Societies, and one representative each from the Commissariats of Supply, Ways of Communication, Labour, Agriculture, Finance, Trade and Industry, and Internal Affairs. It meets as a whole at least once in every month. The work of its members is directed by a Presidium of nine members, of which it elects eight, the President being elected by the All–n Central Executive Committee, and enjoying the rank of a People's Commissar or Minister.

I had a long talk with Rykov, the President, or rather listened to a long lecture by him, only now and then succeeding in stopping him by forcing a question into the thread of his harangue. He stammers a little, and talks so indistinctly that for the first time (No. The first time was when Chicherin gabbled through the provisions of the Brest Treaty at the fourth All–n Assembly.) I felt willing to forgive normal ns, who nearly always talk as if they were in Petrograd and their listener in Vladivostok.

Part of what he said is embodied in what I have already written. But besides sketching the general aims of the Council, Rykov talked of the present economic position of . At the moment n industry was in peculiar difficulties owing to the fuel crisis. This was partly due to the fact that the Czechs and the Reactionaries, who had used the Czechs to screen their own organization, had control of the coalfields in the Urals, and partly to the fact that the German occupation of the Ukraine and the activities of Krasnov had cut off Soviet from the Donetz coal basin, which had been a main source of supply, although in the old days Petrograd had also got coal from England. It was now, however, clear that, with a friendly Ukraine, they would have the use of the Donetz basin much sooner than they had expected.

The Brest peace and the deprivations it involved had made them consider the position of the industrial districts from a new standpoint, and they were determined to make Petrograd and Moscow as far as possible independent of all fuel which had to be brought from a distance. He referred to the works in progress for utilizing water power to provide electrical energy for the Petrograd factories, and said that similar electrification, on a basis of turf fuel, is planned for Moscow.

I asked how they were going to get the machines. He said that of course they would prefer to buy them abroad, but that, though this was impossible, the work would not be delayed on that account, since they could make a start with the machines they had. Turbines for the Petrograd works they still hoped to obtain from abroad when peace had been arranged. If the worst came to the worst he thought they could make their own. "That is one unexpected result of 's long isolation. Her dependence on imports from abroad is lessening." He gave an example in salt, the urgent need of which has led to the opening of a new industry, whose resources are such as to enable not only to supply herself with salt, but the rest of the world as well if need should be.

I asked what were their immediate plans with regard to the electrification of Moscow. He said that there was no water power near Moscow but big turf deposits which would be used as fuel. In order not to interfere with the actual lighting of the town from the power–station already in existence, they are taking the electric plant from the Provodnik works, which will supply enough electricity for the lighting of the town. As soon as that is set up and working, they will use it for the immediate needs of Moscow, and set about transferring the existing power–station to the new situation near the turf beds. In this way they hope to carry out the change from coal to turf without interfering with the ordinary life of the town. Eventually when things settle down they will get a larger plant.

I said, "Of course you have a double object in this, not only to lessen the dependence of the industrial districts on fuel that has to be brought from a distance, and of which you may be deprived, but also to lessen the strain on transport!"

"Yes," he said. "Indeed at the present moment the latter is our greatest difficulty, hampering everything we would wish to do. And transport we cannot put right without help from abroad. Therefore we do everything we can to use local resources, and are even developing the coal deposits near Moscow, which are of inferior quality to the Donetz coal, and were in the old days purposely smothered by the Donetz coal—owners, who wished to preserve their monopoly."

I asked him if in his opinion could organize herself without help from abroad. He said, "I rather think she will have to. We want steam dredgers, steam excavators, and locomotives most of all, but we have small hope of getting them in the immediate future, because the effects of the war have been so serious in the disorganization of industry in the western countries that it is doubtful whether they will be in a position to supply even their own needs."

While we were talking Berg, the secretary, came in. I asked him how his Soviet matches were progressing, and he said that the labels were being printed and that the first lot would soon be ready. They will be distributed on the card system, and he had calculated that they could sell them at twelve kopecks a packet. I paid a rouble for a box of ordinary matches at Bieloostrov, and a rouble and a half here.

THE RACE WITH RUIN

After leaving Rykov I went to see Krestinsky, the Commissar of Finance, the curious little optimist whose report on the Extraordinary Tax I had heard at the last meeting of the Executive Committee. I found him in the Ilyinka street, in the Chinese town. I began by telling him that I did not believe that they meant to pay the loans. He laughed and gave me precisely the answer I had expected:— "Of course we hope there will be a revolution in other countries, in which case they will repudiate their debts and forgive us ours. But if that does not happen we know very well that we shall have to pay, and we are prepared to pay, and shall be able to pay, in concessions, in raw material which they need more than they need gold."

Then, being myself neither an economist nor a theoretical socialist, I put before him what had been said to me in Stockholm by an Englishman who was both one and the other; namely, that, being isolated from European finance, the Soviet Government of was bound to come to an end on economic and financial grounds alone.

He said: "That would certainly be so, if rising prices, rising wages, were to mean indefinitely increased demands on the printing machines for paper money. But, while we are at present forced to print more and more money, another process is at work which, in the long run, will bring this state of things to an end. Just as in our dealings with other countries we exchange goods instead of paying in money, so within our own frontiers money is ceasing to be the sole medium of exchange. Gradually the workmen are coming to receive more and more in other forms than money. Houses, for example, lighting and heating are only a beginning. These things being state monopolies, the task of supplying the workman's needs without the use of money is comparatively easy. The chief difficulty is, of course, food supplies, which depend on our ability to keep up an exchange of goods with the villages. If we can supply the villages with manufactured goods, they will supply us with food. You can fairly say that our ruin or salvation depends on a race between the decreasing value of money (with the consequent need for printing notes in ever greater quantities) and our growing ability to do without money altogether. That is of course, a broad view, and you must not for a moment suppose that we expect to do without money in the immediate future. I am merely showing you the two opposing tendencies on which our economic fate depends."

I will not set down here what he said about the Extraordinary Tax, for it was merely a repetition of what I had heard him say in committee. In connection with it, however, he admitted that capitalism and profiteering were hard things to root out, saying that they had great difficulty in getting at what he called "the new bourgeoisie," namely the speculators who have made fortunes since the revolution by selling scarce food products at fantastic prices. It was difficult to tax them because they carried on their operations secretly and it was next to impossible to find out who they were. They did not bank their money, and though an attempt had been made to get at them through the house committees, it was found that even these committees were unable to detect them. They will, however, be made to disgorge their ill-gotten gains when the measure first proposed by Sokolnikov last summer is put into practice. This is a general exchange of new money for old, after which the old will be declared invalid. "Of course," said Krestinsky, "they will cheat in every possible way, scattering out the money among a number of friends and relations. But something will have been done in cleaning them up, and that process will be completed by a second exchange of money later on."

Fifteen milliards of new notes for the first exchange are already printed, but they think that twenty milliards will be necessary.

I asked if the new money was better looking than the old, if it looked more like money that was worth having than the wretched little notes printed by the Provisional Government and scornfully called "Kerenkies" by the populace. Krestinsky said he was afraid not, but that the second and final exchange would be made in notes which they expected to be permanent. They did not expect the notes of the first exchange to circulate abroad, but the notes of the second would carry with them state obligation and they expected them to go into general currency. He added, smiling that the words "Proletariat of all lands, unite," were to appear on the notes in eight languages. The question of the look of the notes, of their ability to inspire confidence by their mere appearance, is of real importance in a country where so many of the peasantry will judge their value by nothing else.

I reminded him of the hostility roused in some villages by mistakes in the assessment and collecting of the Extraordinary Tax, mistakes which (so other Communists had assured me) would cost them more, politically, than the tax was worth to them, and asked him, "Will you not have great difficulty in getting the exchange made, and are you not running the risk of providing the reactionaries with a new profitable basis of agitation?"

He said that of course they would not make the attempt unless they felt sure they were politically strong enough to carry it through. "If it is properly explained to the villages there will be nothing to fear, because the measure will not threaten any but the rich and therefore the small minority of the peasantry. It would be a different matter if the same thing were to be tried by the counter–revolutionaries, because they would not discriminate in favour of the poor. If Kolchak and Company overthrow us and try to substitute their money for ours, their action would affect rich and poor alike, minority and majority together. If there were not a hundred other causes guaranteeing the insecurity of their position, the fact that they will be unable to get rid of our money without rousing the most violent opposition in the masses throughout the country would alone be sufficient to do it."

I asked whether that was the reason why they intended to print on the notes "Proletariat of all lands, unite," so that the counter–revolutionaries, unable to tolerate money bearing that hated phrase, should be forced to a step disastrous for themselves.

He laughed, and said that he did not think counter–revolution in the least likely unless brought in by invasion, which he did not think politically possible.

A PLAY OF CHEKHOV

February 21st.

I saw Chekhov's "Uncle Vanya" acted by the cast of the Art Theatre in the First Studio. This is a little theatre holding just over 200 people. It was of course full. It was curious to see how complete the revolution had been in a social sense. It was impossible to tell to what class in pre–revolutionary days any particular member of the audience had belonged. I was struck by the new smartness of the boy officers of the Red Army, of whom a fair number were present. As we waited for the curtain to rise, I thought how the mental attitude of the people had changed. A year ago, we lived with exhilaration or despair on a volcano which might any day erupt and sweep away the new life before any one had become accustomed to live it. Now the danger to the revolution was a thousand miles away on the various fronts. Here, in the centre, the revolution was an established fact. People had ceased to wonder when it would end, were settling into their places in the new social order, and took their pleasures not as if they were plucking flowers on their way to execution, but in the ordinary routine of life.

The play is well known, a drama of bourgeois society in a small country place. A poor landowner scraping money for an elder brother in the town, realizing at last that the brother was not the genius for whom such sacrifice was worth while; a doctor with a love for forestry and dreams of the future; the old mock–genius's young wife; his sister; his adoring mother; the old nurse and the ancient dependent adopted, as it were, with the estate; all these people in their own way make each other suffer. Chekhov's irony places before us wasted lives, hopelessness, exaggerated interest in personalities, vain strugglings after some better outlet for the expression of selves not worth expressing.

That play, acted to–day, seemed as remote as a play of the old regime in France would have seemed five years ago. A gulf seemed to have passed. The play had become a play of historical interest; the life it represented had gone for ever. People in no longer have time for private lives of such a character. Such people no longer exist; some of them have been swept into the flood–tide of revolution and are working as they never hoped to have the chance to work; others, less generous, have been broken and thrown aside. The revolution has been hard on some, and has given new life to others. It has swept away that old life so absolutely that, come what may, it will be a hundred years at least before anywhere in people will be able to be unhappy in that particular way again.

The subject of "Uncle Vanya" was a great deal more remote from the n audience of today than was the opera of "Samson and Delilah" which I heard last week. And, if I realized that the revolution had come to stay, if I realized that Chekhov's play had become a play of historical interest, I realized also that Chekhov was a great master in that his work carried across the gulf between the old life and the new, and affected a revolutionary audience of to–day as strongly as it affected that very different audience of a few years ago. Indeed, the play seemed almost to have gained by the revolution, which had lent it, perhaps, more irony than was in Chekhov's mind as he wrote. Was this the old life? I thought, as I stepped out into the snow. If so, then thank God it has gone!

THE CENTRO–TEXTILE

February 22nd.

This morning I drove to the Dielovoi Dvor, the big house on the Varvarskaya Square which is occupied by the central organization of the textile industry. The head of this organization is Nogin, an extremely capable, energetic n, so capable, indeed, that I found it hard to believe he could really be a n. He is a big man, with a mass of thick brown shaggy hair, so thick that the little bald patch on the top of his head seems like an artificial tonsure. Nogin sketched the lines on which the n textile industry was being reorganized, and gave orders that I should be supplied with all possible printed matter in which to find the details.

The "Centro–Textile" is the actual centre of the economic life of , because, since textiles are the chief materials of exchange between the towns and the villages, on its success depends the success of everything else. The textile industry is, in any case, the most important of all n, industries. Before the war it employed 500,000 workmen, and Nogin said that in spite of the disorganization of the war and of the revolution 400,000 are employed to–day. This may be so in the sense that 400,000 are receiving pay, but lack of fuel or of raw material must have brought many factories to a standstill.

All the big factories have been nationalized. Formerly, although in any one town there might be factories carrying out all the different processes, these factories belonged to different owners. A single firm or bank might control factories scattered over and, so that the whole process should be in its hands, the raw material travelled from factory to factory through the country, instead of merely moving about a single town. Thus a roll of material might have gone through one process at Jaroslav, another at Moscow, and a third at Tula, and finally come back to Jaroslav to be finished, simply because the different factories which worked upon it, though widely scattered, happened to be under one control. Nationalization has made possible the rational regrouping of factories so that the complete process is carried out in one place, consequently saving transport. There are twenty–three complete groups of this kind, and in the textile industry generally about fifty groups in all.

There has been a similar concentration of control. In the old days there were hundreds of different competitive firms with their buildings and offices in the Ilyinka, the Varvarka, and the Nikolskaya.* [(*)Streets and a district in Moscow] The Chinese town* [(*) See above.]was a mass of little offices of different textile firms. The whole of that mass of struggling competitive units of direction had now been concentrated in the house in which we were talking. The control of the workers had been carried through in such a way that the technical experts had proper weight. (See p. 171.) There were periodical conferences of elected representatives of all the factories, and Nogin believed that the system of combined elective workmen's and appointed experts' representation could hardly be improved upon.

Nationalization had had the effect of standardizing the output. Formerly, an infinite variety of slightly different stuffs were produced, the variations being often merely for the sake of being different in the competitive trade. Useless varieties had now been done away with, with the result of greater economy in production.

I asked what he could tell me about their difficulties in the matter of raw material. He said they no longer get anything from America, and while the railway was cut at Orenburg by the Cossacks, they naturally could get no cotton from Turkestan. In fact, last autumn they had calculated that they had only enough material to keep the factories going until December. Now they found they could certainly keep going to the end of March, and probably longer. Many small factories, wishing to make their cases out worse than they were, had under–estimated their stocks. Here, as in other things, the isolation of the revolution had the effect of teaching the ns that they were less dependent upon the outside world than they had been in the habit of supposing. He asked me if I knew it had been considered impossible to combine flax and cotton in such a way that the mixture could be worked in machines intended for cotton only. They had an infinite supply of flax, much of which in the old days had been exported. Investigations carried on for the Centro–Textile by two professors, the brothers Chilikin, had ended in the discovery of three different processes for the cottonizing of flax in such a way that they could now mix not only a small percentage of their flax with cotton and use the old machines, but were actually using fifty per cent. flax and had already produced material experimentally with as much as seventy–five per cent.

(Some days later two young technicians from the Centro–Textile brought me a neatly prepared set of specimens illustrating these new processes and asked me to bring them anything of the same sort from England in return. They were not Bolsheviks—were, in fact, typical non–politicals. They were pleased with what the Centro—Textile was doing, and said that more encouragement was given to research than ever formerly. But they were very despondent about the economic position. I could not make them understand why was isolated, and that I might be unable to bring them technical books from England.)

Nogin rather boastfully said that the western linen industry would suffer from the isolation of , whereas in the long run the ns would be able to do without the rest of the world. With, regard to wool, they would have no difficulty now that they were again united with a friendly Ukraine. The silk industry was to be developed in the Astrakhan district where climatic conditions are particularly favourable.

I asked about the fate of the old textile manufacturers and was told that though many had gone abroad many were working in the nationalized factories. The engineering staff, which mostly struck work at the beginning of the revolution, had almost without exception returned, the younger engineers in particular realizing the new possibilities opening before the industry, the continual need of new improvements, and the immediate welcome given to originality of any kind. Apart from the question of food, which was bad for everybody, the social standard of the workers had risen. Thus one of their immediate difficulties was the provision of proper houses. The capitalists and manufacturers kept the workers in barracks. "Now–a–days the men want better dwellings and we mean to give them better. Some have moved into the old houses of the owners and manufacturers, but of course there are not enough of these to go round, and we have extensive plans in the way of building villages and garden cities for the workmen."

I asked Nogin what, in his opinion, was most needed by from abroad, and he said that as far as the textile industries were concerned they wanted machinery. Like every one else to whom I put this question, he said that every industry in would be in a better position if only they had more locomotives. "Some of our factories are stopping now for lack of fuel, and at Saratov, for example, we have masses of raw material which we are unable to get to Moscow."

MODIFICATION IN THE AGRARIAN PROGRAMME

In the afternoon I met Sereda, the Commissar of Agriculture. He insisted that the agrarian policy had been much misrepresented by their enemies for the purposes of agitation. They had no intention of any such idiocy as the attempt to force the peasants to give up private ownership. The establishment of communes was not to be compulsory in any way; it was to be an illustrative means of propaganda of the idea of communal work, not more. The main task before them was to raise the standard of n agriculture, which under the old system was extremely low. By working many of the old estates on a communal system with the best possible methods they hoped to do two things at once: to teach the peasant to realize the advantages of communal labour, and to show him that he could himself get a very great deal more out of his land than he does. "In other ways also we are doing everything we can to give direct help to the small agriculturists. We have mobilized all the agricultural experts in the country. We are issuing a mass of simply written pamphlets explaining better methods of farming."

(I have seen scores of these pamphlets on forestry, potatoes, turf, rotation of crops, and so on, besides the agricultural journals issued by the Commissariat and sent in large quantities to the villages.)

I told Sereda I had heard that the peasants were refusing to sow more than they wanted for their own needs. He said that on the contrary the latest reports gave them the right to hope for a greater sown area this year than ever before, and that even more would have been sown if Denmark had not been prevented from letting them have the seed for which they had actually paid. I put the same question to him that I put to Nogin as to what they most needed; he replied, "Tractors."

FOREIGN TRADE AND MUNITIONS OF WAR

February 25th.

I had a talk in the Metropole with Krasin, who is Commissar for Trade and Industry and also President of the Committee for Supplying the Needs of the Army. He had disapproved of the November Revolution, but last year, when things looked like going badly, he came to from Stockholm feeling that he could not do otherwise than help. He is an elderly man, an engineer, and very much of a European. We talked first of the n plans with regard to foreign trade. All foreign trade, he said, is now concentrated in the hands of the State, which is therefore able to deal as a single customer. I asked how that would apply to purchase, and whether they expected that countries dealing with them would organize committees through which the whole n trade of each such country should similarly pass. Krasin said, "Of course that would be preferable, but only in the case of socialist countries. As things are now it would be very much to our disadvantage. It is better for us to deal with individual capitalists than with a ring. The formation of a committee in England, for example, with a monopoly of trade with , would have the effect of raising prices against us, since we could no longer go from a dear shop to a cheaper one. Besides, as socialists we naturally wish to do nothing to help in the trustification of English manufacturers."

He recognized that foreign trade on any large scale was impossible until their transport had been improved. proposed to do her paying in raw material, in flax, timber, etc., in materials of which she had great quantities although she could not bring them to the ports until her transport should be restored. It would, therefore, be in the foreigner's own interests to help them in this matter. He added that they were confident that in the long run they could, without foreign help, so far restore their transport as to save themselves from starvation; but for a speedy return to normal conditions foreign help was essential.

The other question we touched was that of munitions. I expressed some surprise that they should be able to do so well although cut off from the west. Krasin said that as far as that was concerned they had ample munitions for a long fight. Heavy artillery is not much use for the kind of warfare waged in ; and as for light artillery, they were making and mending their own. They were not bothering with three–inch shells because they had found that the old regime had left scattered about supplies of three–inch shells sufficient to last them several years. Dynamite also they had in enormous quantities. They were manufacturing gunpowder. The cartridge output had trebled since August when Krasin's committee was formed. He thought even as things were they could certainly fight for a year.

THE PROPOSED DELEGATION FROM BERNE

I do not remember the exact date when the proposal of the Berne International Conference to send a Commission of Enquiry to became known in Moscow, but on February 20th everybody who came to see me was talking about it, and from that date the question as to the reception of the delegates was the most urgently debated of all political subjects. Chicherin had replied immediately to Berne, saying that "though they did not consider the Berne Conference either socialist or in any degree representative of the working—class they nevertheless would permit the Commission's journey into , and would give it every opportunity of becoming acquainted from all sides with the state of affairs, just as they would any bourgeois commission directly or indirectly connected with any of the bourgeois governments, even with those then attacking ."

It may well be imagined that a reply in this style infuriated the Mensheviks who consider themselves more or less affiliated to the parties represented at Berne. What, they shrieked, Kautsky not a socialist? To which their opponents replied, "The Government which Kautsky supports keeps Radek in irons in a gaol." But to me the most interesting thing to observe was that Chicherin's reply was scarcely more satisfactory to some of the Communists. It had been sent off before any general consultation, and it appeared that the Communists themselves were widely divided as to the meaning of the proposal. One party believed that it was a first step towards agreement and peace. The other thought it an ingenious ruse by Clemenceau to get "so—called" socialist condemnation of the Bolsheviks as a basis for allied intervention. Both parties were, of course, wrong in so far as they thought the Allied Governments had anything to do with it. Both the French and English delegates were refused passports. This, however, was not known in Moscow until after I left, and by then much had happened. I think the Conference which founded the Third International in Moscow had its origin in a desire to counter any ill effects that might result from the expected visit of the people of Berne.

Litvinov said he considered the sending of the Commission from Berne the most dangerous weapon yet conceived by their opponents. He complained that he had been unable to get either Lenin or Chicherin to realize that this delegation was a preparation for hostilities, not a preparation for peace. "You do not understand that since the beginning of the war there has been a violent struggle between two Internationals, one of which does not believe in revolution while the other does. In this case a group of men already committed to condemn the revolution are coming to pass judgment on it. If they were not to condemn the revolution they would be condemning themselves. Chicherin ought to have put a condition that a delegation of Left Socialists should also come. But he replied within an hour of getting the telegram from Berne. These idiots here think the delegation is coming to seek a ground for peace. It is nothing of the sort. It is bound to condemn us, and the Bourgeois Governments will know how to profit by the criticism, however mild, that is signed by men who still retain authority as socialists. Henderson, for example (Henderson was at first named as one of the delegates, later replaced by MacDonald), will judge simply by whether people are hungry or not. He will not allow for reasons which are not in our control. Kautsky is less dangerous, because, after all, he will look below the obvious." Reinstein remembered the old personal hostility between Lenin and Kautsky, whom Lenin, in a book which Reinstein thought unworthy of him, had roundly denounced as a renegade and traitor. The only man in the delegation who could be counted on for an honest effort to understand was Longuet.

As the days went on, it became clear that the expected visit had provided a new bone of contention between the n parties. The Communists decided that the delegates should not be treated with any particular honour in the way of a reception. The Mensheviks at once set about preparing a triumphal reception on a large scale for the people whom they described as the representatives of genuine socialism. Demian Biedny retorted in an extremely amusing poetic dialogue, representing the Mensheviks rehearsing their parts to be ready for the reception. Other Communists went to work to prepare a retort of a different kind. They arranged a house for the Berne delegates to live in, but at the same time they prepared to emphasize the difference between the two Internationals by the calling of an anti-Berne conference which should disclaim all connection with that old International which they considered had gone into political bankruptcy at the outbreak of the European war.

THE EXECUTIVE COMMITTEE ON THE RIVAL PARTIES

February 26th.

In the afternoon I got to the Executive Committee in time to hear the end of a report by Rykov on the economic position. He said there was hope for a satisfactory conclusion to the negotiations for the building of the Obi–Kotlas railway, and hoped that this would soon be followed by similar negotiations and by other concessions. He explained that they did not want capitalism in but that they did want the things that capital could give them in exchange for what they could give capital. This was, of course, referring to the opposition criticism that the Soviet was prepared to sell into the hands of the "Anglo–American Imperialistic bandits." Rykov said that the main condition of all concessions would be that they should not effect the international structure of the Soviet Republic and should not lead to the exploitation of the workmen. They wanted railways, locomotives, and machines, and their country was rich enough to pay for these things out of its natural resources without sensible loss to the state or the yielding of an inch in their programme of internal reconstruction.

He was followed by Krestinsky, who pointed out that whereas the commissariats were, in a sense, altered forms of the old ministries, links with the past, the Council of Public Economy, organizing the whole production and distribution of the country, building the new socialist state, was an entirely new organ and a link, not with the past, but with the future.

The two next speeches illustrated one of the main difficulties of the revolution. Krasin (see p. 153) criticized the council for insufficient confidence in the security of the revolution. He said they were still hampered by fears lest here or there capitalism should creep in again. They were unnecessarily afraid to make the fullest possible use of specialists of all kinds who had taken a leading part in industry under the old regime and who, now that the old regime, the old system, had been definitely broken, could be made to serve the new. He believed that unless the utmost use was made of the resources of the country in technical knowledge, etc., they could not hope to organize the maximum productivity which alone could save them from catastrophe.

The speaker who followed him, Glebov, defended precisely the opposite point of view and represented the same attitude with regard to the reorganization of industry as is held by many who object to Trotsky's use of officers of the old army in the reorganization of the new, believing that all who worked in high places under the old regime must be and remain enemies of the revolution, so that their employment is a definite source of danger. Glebov is a trade union representative, and his speech was a clear indication of the non—political undercurrent towards the left which may shake the Bolshevik position and will most certainly come into violent conflict with any definitely bourgeois government that may be brought in by counter—revolution.

In the resolution on the economic position which was finally passed unanimously, one point reads as follows: "It is necessary to strive for just economic relations with other countries in the form of state regulated exchange of goods and the bringing of the productive forces of other countries to the working out of the untouched natural resources of Soviet ." It is interesting to notice the curiously mixed character of the opposition. Some call for "a real socialism," which shall make no concessions whatsoever to foreign capital, others for the cessation of civil war and peace with the little governments which have obtained Allied support. In a single number of the Printers' Gazette, for example, there was a threat to appeal against the Bolsheviks to the delegation from Berne and an attack on Chicherin for being ready to make terms with the Entente.

The next business on the programme was the attitude to be adopted towards the repentant Social Revolutionaries of the Right. Kamenev made the best speech I have ever heard from him, for once in a way not letting himself be drawn into agitational digressions, but going point by point through what he had to say and saying it economically. The S.R.'s had had three watchwords: "War and alliance with the Allies," "Coalition with the bourgeoisie," and "The Constituent Assembly." For over a year they had waged open war with the Soviet Government over these three points. They had been defeated in the field. But they had suffered a far more serious moral defeat in having to confess that their very watchwords had been unsound. "War and Alliance with the Allies" had shown itself to mean the occupation of n territory by foreign troops in no way concerned to save the revolution, but ready, as they had shown, to help every force that was working for its suppression. "Coalition with the Bourgeoisie" had shown itself to be a path the natural ending to which was the dictatorship of the bourgeoisie through military force. "The Constituent Assembly" had been proved to be no more than a useful mask behind which the enemies of the revolution could prepare their forces and trick the masses to their own undoing.

He read the declaration of the Right Social Revolutionaries, admitting that the Soviet Government was the only force working against a dictatorship of the bourgeoisie, and calling upon their troops to overthrow the usurping governments in Siberia, and elsewhere. This repentance, however, had come rather late and there were those who did not share it. He said finally that the Executive Committee must remember that it was not a party considering its relations with another party, but an organ of government considering the attitude of the country towards a party which in the most serious moment of n history had admittedly made grave mistakes and helped 's enemies. Now, in this difficult moment, every one who was sincerely ready to help the working masses of in their struggle had the right to be given a place in the ranks of the fighters. The Social Revolutionaries should be allowed to prove in deeds the sincerity of their recantation. The resolution which was passed recapitulated the recantations, mentioned by name the members of the party with whom discussions had been carried on, withdrew the decision of June 14th (excluding the S.R.'s from the Executive Committee on the ground of their counter–revolutionary tendencies) with regard to all groups of the party which held themselves bound by the recently published declarations, gave them the right equally with other parties to share in the work of the Soviets, and notified the administrative and judicial organs of the Republic to free the arrested S.R.'s who shared the point of view expressed in the recantations. The resolution was passed without enthusiasm but without opposition.

There followed the reading by Avanesov of the decree concerning the Menshevik paper Vsegda Vpered ("Forever Forward," but usually described by critics of the Mensheviks as "Forever Backward"). The resolution pointed out that in spite of the Mensheviks having agreed on the need of supporting the Soviet Government they were actually carrying on an agitation, the effect of which could only be to weaken the army. An example was given of an article, "Stop the Civil War," in which they had pointed out that the war was costing a great deal, and that much of the food supplies went to the army. On these grounds they had demanded the cessation of the civil war. The Committee pointed out that the Mensheviks were making demagogic use of the difficulties of the food supply, due in part to the long isolation from the Ukraine, the Volga district and Siberia, for which those Mensheviks who had worked with the White Guard were themselves partly responsible. They pointed out that was a camp besieged from all sides, that Kolchak had seized the important centre of Perm, that Petrograd was threatened from Finland, that in the streets of Rostov and Novo Tcherkassk gallows with the bodies of workmen were still standing, that Denikin was making a destructive raid in the northern

Caucasus, that the Polish legionaries were working for the seizure of Vilna and the suppression of Lithuania and the White n proletariat, and that in the ports of the Black Sea the least civilized colonial troops of the Entente were supporting the White Guards. They pointed out that the Soviet Government had offered concessions in order to buy off the imperialistic countries and had received no reply. Taking all this into consideration the demand to end civil war amounted to a demand for the disarming of the working class and the poor peasantry in the face of bandits and executioners advancing from all sides. In a word, it was the worst form of state crime, namely, treason to a state of workers and peasants. The Committee considered useful every kind of practical criticism of the work of the Soviet Government in all departments, but it could not allow that in the rear of the Red Army of workers and peasants, under that army's protection, should be carried on unrestrained an agitation which could have only one result, the weakening of Soviet in the face of its many enemies. Therefore Vsegda Vpered would be closed until the Mensheviks should show in deed that they were ready to stand to the defence and support of the revolution. At the same time, the Committee reminded the Mensheviks that a continuation of their counter–revolutionary work would force the Soviet Government "to expel them to the territories of Kolchak's democracy." This conclusion was greeted with laughter and applause, and with that the meeting ended.

COMMISSARIAT OF LABOUR

February 28th.

This morning I went round to the Commissariat of Labour, to see Schmidt, the Commissar. Schmidt is a clean–shaven, intelligent young man, whose attention to business methods is reflected in his Commissariat, which, unlike that of Foreign Affairs, is extremely clean and very well organized. I told him I was particularly interested to hear what he could say in answer to the accusations made both by the Mensheviks and by the Extremists on the Left that control by the workers has become a dead letter, and that a time will come when the trades unions will move against the state organizations.

Schmidt answered: "Those accusations and suggestions are all very well for agitational purposes, but the first to laugh at them would be the trades unions themselves. This Commissariat, for example, which is the actual labour centre, is controlled directly by the unions. As Commissar of Labour, I was elected directly by the General Council of the

Trades Unions. Of the College of nine members which controls the whole work of the Commissariat, five are elected directly by the General Council of the Trades Unions and four appointed by the Council of People's Commissaries, thus giving the Unions a decisive majority in all questions concerning labour. All nine are confirmed by the Council of People's Commissaries, representing the state as a whole, and the Commissar is confirmed by the All–n Executive Committee."

Of course control by the workers, as it was first introduced, led speedily to many absurdities and, much to the dissatisfaction of the extremer elements, has been considerably modified. It was realized that the workers in any particular factory might by considering only their own interests harm the community as a whole, and so, in the long run, themselves. The manner of its modification is an interesting example of the way in which, without the influence of tanks, aeroplanes or bayonets, the cruder ideas of communism are being modified by life. It was reasoned that since the factory was the property, not of the particular workmen who work in it, but of the community as a whole, the community as a whole should have a considerable voice in its management. And the effect of that reasoning has been to ensure that the technical specialist and the expert works manager are no longer at the caprice of a hastily called gathering of the workmen who may, without understanding them, happen to disapprove of some of their dispositions. Thus the economical, administrative council of a nationalized factory consists of representatives of the workmen and clerical staff, representatives of the higher technical and commercial staffs, the directors of the factory (who are appointed by the Central Direction of National Factories), representatives of the local council of trades unions, the Council of Public Economy, the local soviet, and the industrial union of the particular industry carried on in the factory, together with, a representative of the workers' co–operative society and a representative of the peasants' soviet of the district in which the factory is situated. In this council not more than half of the members may be representatives of the workmen and clerical staff of the factory. This council considers the internal order of the factory, complaints of any kind, and the material and moral conditions of work and so on. On questions of a technical character it has no right to do more than give advice.

The night before I saw Schmidt, little Finberg had come to my room for a game of chess in a very perturbed state of mind, having just come from a meeting of the union to which he belonged (the union of clerks, shop assistants and civil servants) where there had been a majority against the Bolsheviks after some fierce criticism over this particular question.

Finberg had said that the ground basis of the discontent had been the lack of food, but that the outspoken criticism had taken the form, first, of protests against the offer of concessions in Chicherin's Note of February 4th, on the ground that concessions meant concessions to foreign capitalism and the formation in of capitalist centres which would eventually spread; and second, that the Communists themselves, by their modifications of Workers' Control, were introducing State Capitalism instead of Socialism.

I mentioned this union to Schmidt, and asked him to explain its hostility. He laughed, and said: "Firstly, that union is not an industrial union at all, but includes precisely the people whose interests are not identical with those of the workmen. Secondly, it includes all the old civil servants who, as you remember, left the ministries at the November Revolution, in many cases taking the money with them. They came back in the end, but though no longer ready to work openly against the revolution as a whole, they retain much of their old dislike of us, and, as you see, the things they were objecting to last night were precisely the things which do not concern them in particular. Any other stick would be as good to them. They know well that if they were to go on strike now they would be a nuisance to us, no more. If you wish to know the attitude of the Trades Unions, you should look at the Trades Union Congress which wholly supported us, and gave a very different picture of affairs. They know well that in all questions of labour, the trades unions have the decisive voice. I told you that the unions send a majority of the members of the College which controls the work of this Commissariat. I should have added that the three most important departments—the department for safeguarding labour, the department for distributing labour, and that for regulating wages—are entirely controlled by the Unions."

"How do politics affect the Commissariat?"

"Not at all. Politics do not count with us, just because we are directly controlled by the Unions, and not, by any political party. Mensheviks, Maximalists and others have worked and are working in the Commissariat. Of course if a man were opposed to the revolution as a whole we should not have him here, because he would be working against us instead of helping."

I asked whether he thought the trade unions would ever disappear in the Soviet organizations. He thought not. On the contrary, they had grown steadily throughout the revolution. He told me that one great change had been made in them. Trade unions have been merged together into industrial unions, to prevent conflict between individual sections of one industry. Thus boilermakers and smiths do not have separate unions, but are united in the metal–workers' union. This unification has its effect on reforms and changes. An increase in wages, for example, is simultaneous all over . The price of living varies very considerably in different parts of the country, there being as great differences between the climates of different parts as there are between the countries of Europe. Consequently a uniform absolute increase would be grossly unfair to some and grossly favourable to others. The increase is therefore proportional to the cost of living. Moscow is taken as a norm of 100, and when a new minimum wage is established for Moscow other districts increase their minimum wage proportionately. A table for this has been worked out, whereby in comparison with 100 for Moscow, Petrograd is set down as 120, Voronezh or Kursk as 70, and so on.

We spoke of the new programme of the Communists, rough drafts of which were being printed in the newspapers for discussion, and he showed me his own suggestions in so far as the programme concerned labour. He wished the programme to include, among other aims, the further mechanization of production, particularly the mechanization of all unpleasant and dirty processes, improved sanitary inspection, shortening of the working day in employments harmful to health, forbidding women with child to do any but very light work, and none at all for eight weeks before giving birth and for eight weeks afterwards, forbidding overtime, and so on. "We have already gone far beyond our old programme, and our new one steps far ahead of us. is the first country in the world where all workers have a fortnight's holiday in the year, and workers in dangerous or unhealthy occupations have a month's."

I said, "Yes, but don't you find that there is a very long way between the passing of a law and its realization?"

Schmidt laughed and replied: "In some things certainly, yes. For example, we are against all overtime, but, in the present state of we should be sacrificing to a theory the good of the revolution as a whole if we did not allow and encourage overtime in transport repairs. Similarly, until things are further developed than they are now, we should be criminal slaves to theory if we did not, in some cases, allow lads under sixteen years old to be in the factories when we have not yet been able to provide the necessary schools where we would wish them to be. But the programme is there, and as fast as it can be realized we are realizing it."

EDUCATION

February 28th.

At the Commissariat of Public Education I showed Professor Pokrovsky a copy of The German–Bolshevik Conspiracy, published in America, containing documents supposed to prove that the German General Staff arranged the November Revolution, and that the Bolsheviks were no more than German agents. The weak point about the documents is that the most important of them have no reason for existence except to prove that there was such a conspiracy. These are the documents bought by Mr. Sisson. I was interested to see what Pokrovsky would say of them. He looked through them, and while saying that he had seen forged documents better done, pointed as evidence to the third of them which ends with the alleged signatures of Zalkind, Polivanov, Mekhinoshin and Joffe. He observed that whoever forged the things knew a good deal, but did not know quite enough, because these persons, described as "plenipotentiaries of the Council of Peoples' Commissars," though all actually in the service of the Soviet Government, could not all, at that time, have been what they were said to be. Polivanov, for example, was a very minor official. Joffe, on the other: hand, was indeed a person of some importance. The putting of the names in that order was almost as funny as if they had produced a document signed by Lenin and the Commandant of the Kremlin, putting the latter first.

Pokrovsky told me a good deal about the organization of this Commissariat, as Lunacharsky, the actual head of it, was away in Petrograd. The routine work is run by a College of nine members appointed by the Council of People's Commissars. The Commissar of Education himself is appointed by the All–n Executive Committee. Besides this, there is a Grand College which meets rarely for the settlement of important questions. In it are representatives of the Trades Unions, the Workers' Co–operatives, the Teachers' Union, various Commissariats such as that for affairs of Nationality, and other public organizations. He also gave me then and at a later date a number of figures illustrating the work that has been done since the revolution. Thus whereas there used to be six universities there are now sixteen, most of the new universities having been opened on the initiative of the local Soviets, as at Astrakhan, Nijni, Kostroma, Tambov, Smolensk and other places. New polytechnics are being founded. At Ivano–Vosnesensk the new polytechnic is opened and that at Briansk is being prepared. The number of students in the universities has increased enormously though not to the same proportion as the number of universities, partly because the difficulties of food supply keep many students out of the towns, and partly because of the newness of some of the universities which are only now gathering their students about them. All education is free. In August last a decree was passed abolishing preliminary examinations for persons wishing to become students. It was considered that very many people who could attend the lectures with profit to themselves had been prevented by the war or by pre–revolution conditions from acquiring the sort of knowledge that could be tested by examination. It was also believed that no one would willingly listen to lectures that were of no use to him. They hoped to get as many working men into the universities as possible. Since the passing of that decree the number of students at Moscow University, for example, has more than doubled. It is interesting to notice that of the new students a greater number are studying in the faculties of science and history and philosophy than in those of medicine or law. Schools are being unified on a new basis in which labour plays a great part. I frankly admit I do not understand, and I gather that many teachers have also failed to understand, how this is done. Crafts of all kinds take a big place in the scheme. The schools are divided into two classes—one for children from seven to twelve years old, and one for those aged from thirteen to seventeen. A milliard roubles has been assigned to feeding children in the schools, and those who most need them are supplied with clothes and footgear. Then there are many classes for working men, designed to give the worker a general scientific knowledge of his own trade and so prevent him from being merely a machine carrying out a single uncomprehended process. Thus a boiler–maker can attend a course on mechanical engineering, an electrical worker a course on electricity, and the best agricultural experts are being employed to give similar lectures to the peasants. The workmen crowd to these courses. One course, for example, is attended by a thousand men in spite of the appalling cold of the lecture rooms. The hands of the science professors, so Pokrovsky told me, are frostbitten from touching the icy metal of their instruments during demonstrations.

The following figures represent roughly the growth in the number of libraries. In October, 1917, there were 23 libraries in Petrograd, 30 in Moscow. Today there are 49 in Petrograd and 85 in Moscow, besides a hundred book distributing centres. A similar growth in the number of libraries has taken place in the country districts. In Ousolsky ouezd, for example, there are now 73 village libraries, 35 larger libraries and 500 hut libraries or reading rooms. In Moscow educational institutions, not including schools, have increased from 369 to 1,357.

The in 1919

There are special departments for the circulation of printed matter, and they really have developed a remarkable organization. I was shown over their headquarters on the Tverskaya, and saw huge maps of with all the distributing centres marked with reference numbers so that it was possible to tell in a moment what number of any new publication should be sent to each. Every post office is a distributing centre to which is sent a certain number of all publications, periodical and other. The local Soviets ask through the post offices for such quantities as are required, so that the supply can be closely regulated by the demand. The book–selling kiosks send in reports of the sale of the various newspapers, etc., to eliminate the waste of over–production, a very important matter in a country faced simultaneously by a vigorous demand for printed matter and an extreme scarcity of paper.

It would be interesting to have statistics to illustrate the character of the literature in demand. One thing can be said at once. No one reads sentimental romances. As is natural in a period of tremendous political upheaval pamphlets sell by the thousand, speeches of Lenin and Trotsky are only equalled in popularity by Demian Biedny's more or less political poetry. Pamphlets and books on Marx, on the war, and particularly on certain phases of the revolution, on different aspects of economic reconstruction, simply written explanations of laws or policies vanish almost as soon as they are put on the stalls. The reading of this kind has been something prodigious during the revolution. A great deal of poetry is read, and much is written. It is amusing to find in a red–hot revolutionary paper serious articles and letters by well–meaning persons advising would–be proletarian poets to stick to Pushkin and Lermontov. There is much excited controversy both in magazine and pamphlet form as to the distinguishing marks of the new proletarian art which is expected to come out of the revolution and no doubt will come, though not in the form expected. But the Communists cannot be accused of being unfaithful to the n classics. Even Radek, a foreign fosterchild and an adopted n, took Gogol as well as Shakespeare with him when he went to annoy General Hoffmann at Brest. The Soviet Government has earned the gratitude of many ns who dislike it for everything else it has done by the resolute way in which it has brought the n classics into the bookshops. Books that were out of print and unobtainable, like Kliutchevsky's "Courses in n History," have been reprinted from the stereotypes and set afloat again at most reasonable prices. I was also able to buy a book of his which I have long wanted, his "Foreigners' Accounts of the Muscovite State," which had also fallen out of print. In the same way the Government has reprinted, and sells at fixed low prices that may not be raised by retailers, the works of Koltzov, Nikitin, Krylov, Saltykov–Shtchedrin, Chekhov, Goncharov, Uspensky,

Tchernyshevsky, Pomyalovsky and others. It is issuing Chukovsky's edition of Nekrasov, reprints of Tolstoy, Dostoievsky and Turgenev, and books by Professor Timiriazev, Karl Pearson and others of a scientific character, besides the complete works of Lenin's old rival, Plekhanov. It is true that most of this work is simply done by reprinting from old stereotypes, but the point is that the books are there, and the sale for them is very large.

Among the other experts on the subject of the Soviet's educational work I consulted two friends, a little boy, Glyeb, who sturdily calls himself a Cadet though three of his sisters work in Soviet institutions, and an old and very wise porter. Glyeb says that during the winter they had no heating, so that they sat in school in their coats, and only sat for a very short time, because of the great cold. He told me, however, that they gave him a good dinner there every day, and that lessons would be all right as soon as the weather got warmer. He showed me a pair of felt boots which had been given him at the school. The old porter summed up the similar experience of his sons. "Yes," he said, "they go there, sing the Marseillaise twice through, have dinner and come home." I then took these expert criticisms to Pokrovsky who said, "It is perfectly true. We have not enough transport to feed the armies, let alone bringing food and warmth for ourselves.

And if, under these conditions, we forced children to go through all their lessons we should have corpses to teach, not children. But by making them come for their meals we do two things, keep them alive, and keep them in the habit of coming, so that when the warm weather comes we can do better."

A BOLSHEVIK FELLOW OF THE ROYAL SOCIETY

At Sukhanov's suggestion I went, to see Professor Timiriazev, the greatest n Darwinian, well-known to many scientific men in this country, a foreign member of the Royal Society, a Doctor of Cambridge University and a Bolshevik. He is about eighty years old. His left arm is paralysed, and, as he said, he can only work at his desk and not be out and about to help as he would wish. A venerable old savant, he was sitting writing with a green dressing gown about him, for his little flat was very cold. On the walls were portraits of Darwin, Newton and Gilbert, besides portraits of contemporary men of science whom he had known. English books were everywhere. He gave me, two copies of his last scientific book and his latest portrait to take to two of his friends in England.

He lives with his wife and son. I asked if his son were also a Bolshevik.

"Of course," he replied.

He then read me a letter he had written protesting against intervention. He spoke of his old love for England and for the English people. Then, speaking of the veil of lies drawn between Soviet and the rest of the world, he broke down altogether, and bent his head to hide his tears.

"I suffer doubly," he said, after excusing himself for the weakness of a very old man. "I suffer as a n, and, if I may say so, I suffer as an Englishman. I have English blood in my veins. My mother, you see, looks quite English," pointing to a daguerreotype on the wall, "and my grandmother was actually English. I suffer as an Englishman when I see the country that I love misled by lies, and I suffer as a n because those lies concern the country to which I belong, and the ideas which I am proud to hold."

The old man rose with difficulty, for he, like every one else in Moscow, is half starved. He showed me his Byron, his Shakespeare, his Encyclopaedia Britannica, his English diplomas. He pointed to the portraits on the wall. "If I could but let them know the truth," he said, "those friends of mine in England, they would protest against actions which are unworthy of the England we have loved together."

DIGRESSION

At this point the chronological arrangement of my book, already weak, breaks down altogether. So far I have set down, almost day by day, things seen and heard which seemed to me characteristic and clear illustration of the mentality of the Communists, of the work that has been done or that they are trying to do, and of the general state of affairs. I spent the whole of my time in ceaseless investigation, talking now with this man, now with that, until at the end of a month I was so tired (besides being permanently hungry) that I began to fear rather than to seek new experiences and impressions. The last two weeks of my stay were spent, not in visiting Commissariats, but in collecting masses of printed material, in talking with my friends of the opposition parties, and, while it was in progress, visiting daily the Conference in the Kremlin which, in the end, definitely announced itself as the Third International. I have considered it best to treat of that

Conference more or less as a whole, and am therefore compelled to disregard chronology altogether in putting down on paper, the results of some of my talks with the opposition. Some of these took place on the same days as my visits to the Kremlin conference, and during those days I was also partly engaged in getting to see the British prisoners in the Butyrka prison, in which I eventually succeeded. This is my excuse for the inadequacy of my account of the conference, an inadequacy which I regret the more as I was the only non–Communist who was able to be there at all.

THE OPPOSITION

No man likes being hungry. No man likes being cold. Everybody in Moscow, as in Petrograd, is both hungry and cold. There is consequently very general and very bitter discontent. This is of course increased, not lessened, by the discipline introduced into the factories and the heavy burden of the army, although the one is intended to hasten the end of hunger and cold and the other for the defence of the revolution. The Communists, as the party in power, naturally bear the blame and are the objects of the discontent, which will certainly within a short time be turned upon any other government that may succeed them. That government must introduce sterner discipline rather than weaker, and the transport and other difficulties of the country will remain the same, unless increased by the disorder of a new upheaval and the active or passive resistance of many who are convinced revolutionaries or will become so in answer to repression.

The Communists believe that to let power slip from their hands at this moment would be treachery to the revolution. And, in the face of the advancing forces of the Allies and Kolchak many of the leaders of the opposition are inclined to agree with them, and temporarily to submit to what they undoubtedly consider rank tyranny. A position has been reached after these eighteen months not unlike that reached by the English Parliament party in 1643. I am reminded of a passage in Guizot, which is so illuminating that I make no apology for quoting it in full:—

"The party had been in the ascendant for three years: whether it had or had not, in church and state, accomplished its designs, it was at all events by its aid and concurrence that, for three years, public affairs had been conducted; this alone was sufficient to make many people weary of it; it was made responsible for the many evils already endured, for the many hopes frustrated; it was denounced as being no less addicted to persecution than the bishops, no less arbitrary than the king:]196]its inconsistencies, its weaknesses, were recalled with bitterness; and, independently of this, even without factions or interested views, from the mere progress of events and opinions, there was felt a secret need of new principles and new rulers."

New rulers are advancing on Moscow from Siberia, but I do not think that they claim that they are bringing with them new principles. Though the masses may want new principles, and might for a moment submit to a reintroduction of very old principles in desperate hope of less hunger and less cold, no one but a lunatic could imagine that they would for very long willingly submit to them. In the face of the danger that they may be forced to submit not to new principles but to very old ones, the non–Communist leaders are unwilling to use to the full the discontent that exists. Hunger and cold are a good enough basis of agitation for anyone desirous of overturning any existing government. But the Left Social Revolutionaries, led by the hysterical but flamingly honest Spiridonova, are alone in having no scruples or hesitation in the matter, the more responsible parties fearing the anarchy and consequent weakening of the revolution that would result from any violent change.

THE LEFT SOCIAL REVOLUTIONARIES

The Left Social Revolutionaries want something so much like anarchy that they have nothing to fear in a collapse of the present system. They are for a partisan army, not a regular army. They are against the employment of officers who served under the old regime. They are against the employment of responsible technicians and commercial experts in the factories. They believe that officers and experts alike, being ex–bourgeois, must be enemies of the people, insidiously engineering reaction. They are opposed to any agreement with the Allies, exactly as they were opposed to any agreement with the Germans. I heard them describe the Communists as "the bourgeois gendarmes of the Entente," on the ground that having offered concessions they would be keeping order in for the benefit of Allied capital. They blew up Mirbach, and would no doubt try to blow up any successors he might have. Not wanting a regular army (a low bourgeois weapon) they would welcome occupation in order that they, with bees in their bonnets and bombs in their hands, might go about revolting against it.

I did not see Spiridonova, because on February 11, the very day when I had an appointment with her, the Communists arrested her, on the ground that her agitation was dangerous and anarchist in tendency, fomenting discontent without a programme for its satisfaction. Having a great respect for her honesty, they were hard put to it to know what to do with her, and she was finally sentenced to be sent for a year to a home for neurasthenics, "where she would be able to read and write and recover her normality." That the Communists were right in fearing this agitation was proved by the troubles in Petrograd, where the workmen in some of the factories struck, and passed Left Social Revolutionary resolutions which, so far from showing that they were awaiting reaction and General Judenitch, showed simply that they were discontented and prepared to move to the left.

THE MENSHEVIKS

The second main group of opposition is dominated by the Mensheviks . Their chief leaders are Martov and Dan. Of these two, Martov is by far the cleverer, Dan the more garrulous, being often led away by his own volubility into agitation of a kind not approved by his friends. Both are men of very considerable courage. Both are Jews.

The Mensheviks would like the reintroduction of capitalists, of course much chastened by experience, and properly controlled by themselves. Unlike Spiridonova and her romantic supporters they approved of Chicherin's offer of peace and concessions to the Allies (see page 44). They have even issued an appeal that the Allies should come to an agreement with "Lenin's Government." As may be gathered from their choice of a name for the Soviet Government, they are extremely hostile to it, but they fear worse things, and are consequently a little shy of exploiting as they easily could the dislike of the people for hunger and cold. They fear that agitation on these lines might well result in anarchy, which would leave the revolution temporarily defenceless against Kolchak, Denikin, Judenitch or any other armed reactionary. Their non–Communist enemies say of the Mensheviks: "They have no constructive programme; they would like a bourgeois government back again, in order that they might be in opposition to it, on the left"

On March 2nd, I went to an election meeting of workers and officials of the Moscow Co–operatives. It was beastly cold in the hall of the University where the meeting was held, and my nose froze as well as my feet. Speakers were announced from the Communists, Internationalists, Mensheviks, and Right Social Revolutionaries. The last–named did not arrive. The Presidium was for the most part non–Communist, and the meeting was about equally divided for and against the Communists. A Communist led off with a very bad speech on the general European situation and to the effect that there was no salvation for except by the way she was going. Lozovsky, the old Internationalist, spoke next, supporting the Bolsheviks' general policy but criticizing their suppression of the press. Then came Dan, the Menshevik, to hear whom I had come. He is a little, sanguine man, who gets very hot as he speaks. He conducted an attack on the whole Bolshevik position combined with a declaration that so long as they are attacked from without he is prepared to support them. The gist of his speech was: 1. He was in favour of fighting Kolchak. 2. But the Bolshevik policy with regard to the peasants will, since as the army grows it must contain more and more peasants, end in the creation of an army with counter–revolutionary sympathies. 3. He objected to the Bolshevik criticism of the Berne, delegation (see page 156) on very curious grounds, saying that though Thomas, Henderson, etc., backed their own Imperialists during the war, all that was now over, and that union with them would help, not hinder, revolution in England and France. 4. He pointed out that "All power to the Soviets" now means "All power to the Bolsheviks," and said that he wished that the Soviets should actually have all power instead of merely supporting the Bolshevik bureaucracy. He was asked for his own programme, but said he had not time to give it. I watched the applause carefully. General dissatisfaction with the present state of affairs was obvious, but it was also obvious that no party would have a chance that admitted its aim was extinction of the Soviets (which Dan's ultimate aim certainly is, or at least the changing of them into non–political industrial organizations) or that was not prepared to fight against reaction from without.

I went to see Sukhanov (the friend of Gorky and Martov, though his political opinions do not precisely agree with those of either), partly to get the proofs of his first volume of reminiscences of the revolution, partly to hear what he had to say. I found him muffled up in a dressing gown or overcoat in an unheated flat, sitting down to tea with no sugar, very little bread, a little sausage and a surprising scrap of butter, brought in, I suppose, from the country by a friend. Nikitsky, a Menshevik, was also there, a hopeless figure, prophesying the rotting of the whole system and of the revolution. Sukhanov asked me if I had noticed the disappearance of all spoons (there are now none, but wooden spoons in the Metropole) as a symbol of the falling to pieces of the revolution. I told him that though I had not lived in thirty years or more, as he had, I had yet lived there long enough and had, before the revolution, sufficient experience in the loss of fishing tackle, not to be surprised that n peasants, even delegates, when able, as in such a moment of convulsion as the revolution, stole spoons if only as souvenirs to show that they had really been to Moscow.

We talked, of course, of their attitude towards the Bolsheviks. Both work in Soviet institutions. Sukhanov (Nikitsky agreeing) believed that if the Bolsheviks came further to meet the other parties, Mensheviks, etc., "Kolchak and Denikin would commit suicide and your Lloyd George would give up all thought of intervention." I asked, What if they should be told to hold a Constituent Assembly or submit to a continuance of the blockade? Sukhanov said, "Such a Constituent Assembly would be impossible, and we should be against it." Of the Soviets, one or other said, "We stand absolutely on the platform of the Soviet Government now: but we think that such a form cannot be permanent. We consider the Soviets perfect instruments of class struggle, but not a perfect form of government." I asked Sukhanov if he thought counter revolution possible. He said "No," but admitted that there was a danger lest the agitation of the Mensheviks or others might set fire to the discontent of the masses against the actual physical conditions, and end in pogroms destroying Bolsheviks and Mensheviks alike. Their general theory was that was not so far developed that a Socialist State was at present possible. They therefore wanted a state in which private capital should exist, and in which factories were not run by the state but by individual owners. They believed that the peasants, with their instincts of small property–holders, would eventually enforce something of the kind, and that the end would be some form of democratic Republic. These two were against the offering of concessions to the Allies, on the ground that those under consideration involved the handing over to the concessionaires of the whole power in northern —railways, forests, the right to set up their own banks in the towns served by the railway, with all that this implied. Sukhanov was against concessions on principle, and regretted that the Mensheviks were in favour of them.

I saw Martov at the offices of his newspaper, which had just been suppressed on account of an article, which he admitted was a little indiscreet, objecting to the upkeep of the Red Army (see page 167). He pointed eloquently to the seal on some of the doors, but told me that he had started a new paper, of which he showed me the first number, and told me that the demand for it was such that although he had intended that it should be a weekly he now expected to make it a daily. Martov said that he and his party were against every form of intervention for the following reasons: 1. The continuation of hostilities, the need of an army and of active defence were bound to intensify the least desirable qualities of the revolution whereas an agreement, by lessening the tension, would certainly lead to moderation of Bolshevik Policy. 2. The needs of the army overwhelmed every effort at restoring the economic life of the country. He was further convinced that intervention of any kind favoured reaction, even supposing that the Allies did not wish this. "They cannot help themselves," he said, "the forces that would support intervention must be dominated by those of reaction, since all of the non–reactionary parties are prepared to sink their differences with the Bolsheviks, in order to defend the revolution as a whole." He said he was convinced that the Bolsheviks would either have to alter or go. He read me, in illustration of this, a letter from a peasant showing the unreadiness of the peasantry to go into communes (compulsion in this matter has already been discarded by the Central Government). "We took the land," wrote the peasant in some such words, "not much, just as much as we could work, we ploughed it where it had not been ploughed before, and now, if it is made into a commune, other lazy fellows who have done nothing will come in and profit by our work." Martov argued that life itself, the needs of the country and the will of the peasant masses, would lead to the changes he thinks desirable in the Soviet regime.

THE RIGHT SOCIAL REVOLUTIONARIES

The position of the Right Social Revolutionaries is a good deal more complicated than that of the Mensheviks. In their later declarations they are as far from their romantic anarchist left wing as they are from their romantic reactionary extreme right. They stand, as they have always stood, for a Constituent Assembly, but they have thrown over the idea of instituting a Constituent Assembly by force. They have come into closer contact with the Allies than any other party to the left of the Cadets. By doing so, by associating themselves with the Czech forces on the Volga and minor revolts of a reactionary character inside , they have pretty badly compromised themselves. Their change of attitude towards the Soviet Government must not be attributed to any change in their own programme, but to the realization that the forces which they imagined were supporting them were actually being used to support something a great deal further right. The Printers' Gazette, a non–Bolshevik organ, printed one of their resolutions, one point of which demands the overthrow of the reactionary governments supported by the Allies or the Germans, and another condemns every attempt to overthrow the Soviet Government by force of arms, on the ground that such an attempt would weaken the working class as a whole and would be used by the reactionary groups for their own purposes.

Volsky is a Right Social Revolutionary, and was President of that Conference of Members of the Constituent Assembly from whose hands the Directorate which ruled in Siberia received its authority and Admiral Kolchak his command, his proper title being Commander of the Forces of the Constituent Assembly. The Constituent Assembly members were to have met on January 1st of this year, then to retake authority from the Directorate and organize a government on an All−n basis. But there was continual friction between the Directorate and the Conference of members of the Constituent Assembly, the Directorate being more reactionary than they. In November came Kolchak's coup d'=82tat, followed by a declaration against him and an appeal for his overthrow issued by members of the Constituent Assembly. Some were arrested by a group of officers. A few are said to have been killed. Kolchak, I think, has denied responsibility for this, and probably was unaware of the intentions of the reactionaries under his command. Others of the members escaped to Ufa. On December 5th, 25 days before that town was taken by the Bolsheviks, they announced their intention of no longer opposing the Soviet Government in the field. After the capture of the town by the Soviet troops, negotiations were begun between the representatives of the Conference of Members of the Constituent Assembly, together with other Right Social Revolutionaries, and representatives of the Soviet Government, with a view to finding a basis for agreement. The result of those negotiations was the resolution passed by the Executive Committee on February 26th (see page 166). A delegation of the members came to Moscow, and were quaintly housed in a huge room in the Metropole, where they had put up beds all round the walls and big tables in the middle of the room for their deliberations. It was in this room that I saw Volsky first, and afterwards in my own.

I asked him what exactly had brought him and all that he represented over from the side of Kolchak and the Allies to the side of the Soviet Government. He looked me straight in the face, and said: "I'll tell you. We were convinced by many facts that the policy of the Allied representatives in Siberia was directed not to strengthening the Constituent Assembly against the Bolsheviks and the Germans, but simply to strengthening the reactionary forces behind our backs."

He also complained: "All through last summer we were holding that front with the Czechs, being told that there were two divisions of Germans advancing to attack us, and we now know that there were no German troops in at all."

He criticized the Bolsheviks for being better makers of programmes than organizers. They offered free electricity, and presently had to admit that soon there would be no electricity for lack of fuel. They did not sufficiently base their policy on the study of actual possibilities. "But that they are really fighting against a bourgeois dictatorship is clear to us. We are, therefore, prepared to help them in every possible way."

He said, further: "Intervention of any kind will prolong the regime of the Bolsheviks by compelling us to drop opposition to the Soviet Government, although we do not like it, and to support it because it is defending the revolution."

With regard to help given to individual groups or governments fighting against Soviet , Volsky said that they saw no difference between such intervention and intervention in the form of sending troops.

I asked what he thought would happen. He answered in almost the same words as those used by Martov, that life itself would compel the Bolsheviks to alter their policy or to go. Sooner or later the peasants would make their will felt, and they were against the bourgeoisie and against the Bolsheviks. No bourgeois reaction could win permanently against the Soviet, because it could have nothing to offer, no idea for which people would fight. If by any chance Kolchak, Denikin and Co. were to win, they would have to kill in tens of thousands where the Bolsheviks have had to kill in hundreds, and the result would be the complete ruin and the collapse of in anarchy. "Has not the Ukraine been enough to teach the Allies that even six months' occupation of non−Bolshevik territory by half a million troops has merely the effect of turning the population into Bolsheviks?"

THE THIRD INTERNATIONAL

March 3rd.

One day near the end of February, Bucharin, hearing that I meant to leave quite soon, said rather mysteriously, "Wait a few days longer, because something of international importance is going to happen which will certainly be of interest for your history." That was the only hint I got of the preparation of the Third International. Bucharin refused to say more. On March 3rd Reinstein looked in about nine in the morning and said he had got me a guest's ticket for the conference in the Kremlin, and wondered why I had not been there the day before, when it had opened. I told him I knew nothing whatever about it; Litvinov and Karakhan, whom I had seen quite recently, had never mentioned it, and guessing that this must be the secret at which Bucharin had hinted, I supposed that they had purposely kept silence. I therefore rang up Litvinov, and asked if they had had any reason against my going. He said that he had thought it would not interest me. So I went. The Conference was still a secret. There was nothing about it in the morning papers.

The in 1919

The meeting was in a smallish room, with a dais at one end, in the old Courts of Justice built in the time of Catherine the Second, who would certainly have turned in her grave if she had known the use to which it was being put. Two very smart soldiers of the Red Army were guarding the doors. The whole room, including the floor, was decorated in red. There were banners with "Long Live the Third International" inscribed upon them in many languages. The Presidium was on the raised dais at the end of the room, Lenin sitting in the middle behind a long red–covered table with Albrecht, a young German Spartacist, on the right and Platten, the Swiss, on the left. The auditorium sloped down to the foot of the dais. Chairs were arranged on each side of an alleyway down the middle, and the four or five front rows had little tables for convenience in writing. Everybody of importance was there; Trotzky, Zinoviev, Kamenev, Chichern, Bucharin, Karakhan, Litvinov, Vorovsky, Steklov, Rakovsky, representing here the Balkan Socialist Party, Skripnik, representing the Ukraine. Then there were Stang (Norwegian Left Socialists), Grimlund (Swedish Left), Sadoul (France), Finberg (British Socialist Party), Reinstein (American Socialist Labour Party), a Turk, a German–Austrian, a Chinese, and so on. Business was conducted and speeches were made in all languages, though where possible German was used, because more of the foreigners knew German than knew French. This was unlucky for me.

When I got there people were making reports about the situation in the different countries. Finberg spoke in English, Rakovsky in French, Sadoul also. Skripnik, who, being asked, refused to talk German and said he would speak in either Ukrainian or , and to most people's relief chose the latter, made several interesting points about the new revolution in the Ukraine. The killing of the leaders under the Skoropadsky regime had made no difference to the movement, and town after town was falling after internal revolt. (This was before they had Kiev and, of course, long before they had taken Odessa, both of which gains they confidently prophesied.) The sharp lesson of German occupation had taught the Ukrainian Social Revolutionaries what their experiences during the last fifteen months had taught the n, and all parties were working together.

But the real interest of the gathering was in its attitude towards the Berne conference. Many letters had been received from members of that conference, Longuet for example, wishing that the Communists had been represented there, and the view taken at Moscow was that the left wing at Berne was feeling uncomfortable at sitting down with Scheidemann and Company; let them definitely break with them, finish with the Second International and join the Third. It was clear that this gathering in the Kremlin was meant as the nucleus of a new International opposed to that which had split into national groups, each supporting its own government in the prosecution of the war. That was the leit motif of the whole affair.

Trotsky, in a leather coat, military breeches and gaiters, with a fur hat with the sign of the Red Army in front, was looking very well, but a strange figure for those who had known him as one of the greatest anti—militarists in Europe. Lenin sat quietly listening, speaking when necessary in almost every European language with astonishing ease. Balabanova talked about Italy and seemed happy at last, even in Soviet , to be once more in a "secret meeting." It was really an extraordinary affair and, in spite of some childishness, I could not help realizing that I was present at something that will go down in the histories of socialism, much like that other strange meeting convened in London in 1848.

The vital figures of the conference, not counting Platten, whom I do not know and on whom I can express no opinion, were Lenin and the young German, Albrecht, who, fired no doubt by the events actually taking place in his country, spoke with brain and character. The German Austrian also seemed a real man. Rakovsky, Skripnik, and Sirola the Finn really represented something. But there was a make—believe side to the whole affair, in which the English Left Socialists were represented by Finberg, and the Americans by Reinstein, neither of whom had or was likely to have any means of communicating with his constituents.

March 4th.

In the Kremlin they were discussing the programme on which the new International was to stand. This is, of course, dictatorship of the proletariat and all that that implies. I heard, Lenin make a long speech, the main point of which was to show that Kautsky and his supporters at Berne were now condemning the very tactics which they had praised in 1906. When I was leaving the Kremlin I met Sirola walking in the square outside the building without a hat, without a coat, in a cold so intense that I was putting snow on my nose to prevent frostbite. I exclaimed. Sirola smiled his ingenuous smile. "It is March," he said, "Spring is coming."

March 5th.

Today all secrecy was dropped, a little prematurely, I fancy, for when I got to the Kremlin I found that the first note of opposition had been struck by the man who least of all was expected to strike it. Albrecht, the young German, had opposed the immediate founding of the Third International, on the double ground that not all nations were properly represented and that it might make difficulties for the political parties concerned in their own countries. Every one was against him. Rakovsky pointed out that the same objections could have been raised against the founding of the First International by Marx in London. The German–Austrian combated Albrecht's second point. Other people said that the different parties concerned had long ago definitely broken with the Second International. Albrecht was in a minority of one. It was decided therefore that this conference was actually the Third International. Platten announced the decision, and the "International" was sung in a dozen languages at once. Then Albrecht stood up, a little red in the face, and said that he, of course, recognized the decision and would announce it in Germany.

March 6th.

The conference in the Kremlin ended with the usual singing and a photograph. Some time before the end, when Trotsky had just finished speaking and had left the tribune, there was a squeal of protest from the photographer who had just trained his apparatus. Some one remarked "The Dictatorship of the Photographer," and, amid general laughter, Trotsky had to return to the tribune and stand silent while the unabashed photographer took two pictures. The founding of the Third International had been proclaimed in the morning papers, and an extraordinary meeting in the Great Theatre announced for the evening. I got to the theatre at about five, and had difficulty in getting in, though I had a special ticket as a correspondent. There were queues outside all the doors. The Moscow Soviet was there, the Executive Committee, representatives of the Trades Unions and the Factory Committees, etc. The huge theatre and the platform were crammed, people standing in the aisles and even packed close together in the wings of the stage. Kamenev opened the meeting by a solemn announcement of the founding of the Third International in the Kremlin. There was a roar of applause from the audience, which rose and sang the "International" in a way that I have never heard it sung since the All–n Assembly when the news came of the strikes in Germany during the Brest negotiations. Kamenev then spoke of those who had died on the way, mentioning Liebknecht and Rosa Luxembourg, and the whole theatre stood again while the orchestra played, "You fell as victims." Then Lenin spoke. If I had ever thought that Lenin was losing his personal popularity, I got my answer now. It was a long time before he could speak at all, everybody standing and drowning his attempts to speak with roar after roar of applause. It was an extraordinary, overwhelming scene, tier after tier crammed with workmen, the parterre filled, the whole platform and the wings. A knot of workwomen were close to me, and they almost fought to see him, and shouted as if each one were determined that he should hear her in particular. He spoke as usual, in the simplest way, emphasizing the fact that the revolutionary struggle everywhere was forced to use the Soviet forms. "We declare our solidarity with the aims of the Sovietists," he read from an Italian paper, and added, "and that was when they did not know what our aims were, and before we had an established programme ourselves." Albrecht made a very long reasoned speech for Spartacus, which was translated by Trotsky. Guilbeau, seemingly a mere child, spoke of the socialist movement in France. Steklov was translating him when I left. You must remember that I had had nearly two years of such meetings, and am not a n. When I got outside the theatre, I found at each door a disappointed crowd that had been unable to get in.

The proceedings finished up next day with a review in the Red Square and a general holiday.

If the Berne delegates had come, as they were expected, they would have been told by the Communists that they were welcome visitors, but that they were not regarded as representing the International. There would then have ensued a lively battle over each one of the delegates, the Mensheviks urging him to stick to Berne, and the Communists urging him to express allegiance to the Kremlin. There would have been demonstrations and counter–demonstrations, and altogether I am very sorry that it did not happen and that I was not there to see.

LAST TALK WITH LENIN

I went to see Lenin the day after the Review in the Red Square, and the general holiday in honour of the Third International. The first thing he said was: "I am afraid that the Jingoes in England and France will make use of yesterday's doings as an excuse for further action against us. They will say 'How can we leave them in peace when they set about setting the world on fire?' To that I would answer, 'We are at war, Messieurs! And just as during your war you tried to make revolution in Germany, and Germany did make trouble in Ireland and India, so we, while we are at war with you, adopt the measures that are open to us. We have told you we are willing to make peace.'"

He spoke of Chicherin's last note, and said they based all their hopes on it. Balfour had said somewhere, "Let the fire burn itself out." That it would not do. But the quickest way of restoring good conditions in was, of course, peace and agreement with the Allies. "I am sure we could come to terms, if they want to come to terms at all. England and America would be willing, perhaps, if their hands were not tied by France. But intervention in the large sense can now hardly be. They must have learnt that could never be governed as India is governed, and that sending troops here is the same thing as sending them to a Communist University."

I said something about the general hostility to their propaganda noticeable in foreign countries.

Lenin. "Tell them to build a Chinese wall round each of their countries. They have their customs–officers, their frontiers, their coast–guards. They can expel any Bolsheviks they wish. Revolution does not depend on propaganda. If the conditions of revolution are not there no sort of propaganda will either hasten or impede it. The war has brought about those conditions in all countries, and I am convinced that if today were to be swallowed up by the sea, were to cease to exist altogether, the revolution in the rest of Europe would go on. Put under water for twenty years, and you would not affect by a shilling or an hour a week the demand, of the shop–stewards in England."

I told him, what I have told most of them many times, that I did not believe there would be a revolution in England.

Lenin. "We have a saying that a man may have typhoid while still on his legs. Twenty, maybe thirty years ago I had abortive typhoid, and was going about with it, had had it some days before it knocked me over. Well, England and France and Italy have caught the disease already. England may seem to you to be untouched, but the microbe is already there."

I said that just as his typhoid was abortive typhoid, so the disturbances in England to which he alluded might well be abortive revolution, and come to nothing. I told him the vague, disconnected character of the strikes and the generally liberal as opposed to socialist character of the movement, so far as it was political at all, reminded me of what

91

The in 1919

I had heard of 1905 in and not at all of 1917, and that I was sure it would settle down.

Lenin. "Yes, that is possible. It is, perhaps, an educative period, in which the English workmen will come to realize their political needs, and turn from liberalism to Socialism. Socialism is certainly weak in England. Your socialist movements, your socialist parties . . . when I was in England I zealously attended everything I could, and for a country with so large an industrial population they were pitiable, pitiable . . . a handful at a street corner . . . a meeting in a drawing room . . . a school class . . . pitiable. But you must remember one great difference between of 1905 and England of to–day. Our first Soviet in was made during the revolution. Your shop–stewards committees have been in existence long before. They are without programme, without direction, but the opposition they will meet will force a programme upon them."

Speaking of the expected visit of the Berne delegation, he asked me if I knew MacDonald, whose name had been substituted for that of Henderson in later telegrams announcing their coming. He ,said: "I am very glad MacDonald is coming instead of Henderson. Of course MacDonald is not a Marxist in any sense of the word, but he is at least interested in theory, and can therefore be trusted to do his best to understand what is happening here. More than that we do not ask."

We then talked a little on a subject that interests me very much, namely, the way in which insensibly, quite apart from war, the Communist theories are being modified in the difficult process of their translation into practice. We talked of the changes in "workers' control," which is now a very different thing from the wild committee business that at first made work almost impossible. We talked then of the antipathy of the peasants to compulsory communism, and how that idea also had been considerably whittled away. I asked him what were going to be the relations between the Communists of the towns and the property–loving peasants, and whether there was not great danger of antipathy between them, and said I regretted leaving too soon to see the elasticity of the Communist theories tested by the inevitable pressure of the peasantry.

Lenin said that in there was a pretty sharp distinction between the rich peasants and the poor. "The only opposition we have here in is directly or indirectly due to the rich peasants. The poor, as soon as they are liberated from the political domination of the rich, are on our side and are in an enormous majority."

92

I said that would not be so in the Ukraine, where property among the peasants is much more equally distributed.

Lenin. "No. And there, in the Ukraine, you will certainly see our policy modified. Civil war, whatever happens, is likely to be more bitter in the Ukraine than elsewhere, because there the instinct of property has been further developed in the peasantry, and the minority and majority will be more equal."

He asked me if I meant to return, saying that I could go down to Kiev to watch the revolution there as I had watched it in Moscow. I said I should be very sorry to think that this was my last visit to the country which I love only second to my own. He laughed, and paid me the compliment of saying that, "although English," I had more or less succeeded in understanding what they were at, and that he should be pleased to see me again.

THE JOURNEY OUT

March 15th.

There is nothing to record about the last few days of my visit, fully occupied as they were with the collection and packing of printed material and preparations for departure. I left with the two Americans, Messrs. Bullitt and Steffens, who had come to Moscow some days previously, and travelled up in the train with Bill Shatov, the Commandant of Petrograd, who is not a Bolshevik but a fervent admirer of Prince Kropotkin, for the distribution of whose works in he has probably done as much as any man. Shatov was an emigr=82 in New York, returned to , brought law and order into the chaos of the Petrograd–Moscow railway, never lost a chance of doing a good turn to an American, and with his level–headedness and practical sense became one of the hardest worked servants of the Soviet, although, as he said, the moment people stopped attacking them he would be the first to pull down the Bolsheviks. He went into the occupied provinces during the German evacuation of them, to buy arms and ammunition from the German soldiers. Prices, he said, ran low. You could buy rifles for a mark each, field guns for 150 marks, and a field wireless station for 500. He had then been made Commandant of Petrograd, although there had been some talk of setting him to reorganize transport. Asked how long he thought the Soviet Government could hold but, he replied, "We can

The in 1919

afford to starve another year for the sake of the Revolution."

CPSIA information can be obtained
at www.ICGtesting.com
Printed in the USA
BVHW06s2307230718
522385BV00021B/964/P